D1084681

JOHN WESLEY AND THE
COMING COMPREHENSIVE CHURCH

THE WESLEY HISTORICAL SOCIETY LECTURE
NUMBER THIRTY-THREE

JOHN WESLEY AND THE COMING COMPREHENSIVE CHURCH

FREDERICK HUNTER, M.A., B.D.

LONDON
EPWORTH PRESS

© FREDERICK HUNTER 1968

FIRST PUBLISHED IN 1968

BY EPWORTH PRESS

Book Steward: Frank H. Cumbers

SBN 7162 0036 8

SET IN MONOTYPE IMPRINT AND PRINTED IN
GREAT BRITAIN BY THE CAMELOT PRESS LTD
LONDON AND SOUTHAMPTON

Contents

To Laura

Foreword

Many thanks to the Wesley Historical Society for all the aid it has given to all students of Wesley, and, in particular, for giving me the additional urge to bring a lifetime's interest to focus in this study. Earlier research called for absorbingly interesting detective work, but I did not anticipate the breathtaking interest I have had at times in this further discovery and examination of clues. The result seems to me dramatically relevant at this stage in our current discussions about Union with the Church of England and other Churches. I have never suspected myself of having a fanciful mind, but there has seemed to be something uncanny about the way some material and ideas have come my way. Therefore, whilst thanking a lifelong succession of creditors, and those whose kindnesses are registered in the lecture itself, I salute this other range of experience with similar, yet mystified gratitude.

That fine layman, Mr J. I. Miller of Poole, was prevented by professional responsibilities from presiding over the Lecture, but I thank him for his genuine interest and encouragement. In his absence, the chair was taken by the President of our Society, the Rev. Dr Maldwyn L. Edwards, M.A., who had previously read my manuscript up to the account of Wesley's conversion, and had made useful suggestions. Special mention ought to be made of the Rev. J. C. Bowmer, M.A., B.D., the Rev. G. Herber Davies, B.D., Mr J. M. Ross, M.A., the late Dr G. S. M. Walker of Leeds University, and Dr Williams's and other Libraries. Miss Edith Law has dealt with wonderful success with intricate alterations in typing from my original typescript. And what patience my wife has had in reading much that I have written—and in many other ways!

My space is so limited that I have been content to present Wesley's views—anyway, my own defence of them, or divergence from them, is unimportant in the present discussions. There is ammunition here for those who seek it. Put it down! Look at what remains with Wesley's eyes. He would have it all used in peace. He ever wrote to unite Methodism, and the Church of God. Let us hail him with his own words, 'Peacemaker in the Church of God . . . The God of peace is on your side . . . In due time, thou shalt reap.' Is there, for us, an echo of his accents in the words that often dismiss us from the Table of the Lord, 'Go in peace, and the God of peace go with thee'?

CHAPTER ONE

The Unity and Holiness of the Catholic and Apostolic Church

1725–1733

WE are to consider the influence on the Wesleys of a remarkable group of eighteenth-century Non-Jurors. The original Non-Jurors (Latin 'juro'=I swear) refused to swear the oath of loyalty to William in 1689, for they had formerly pledged their oath to James II who had been deposed. They believed that authority for the Church lay neither in pope nor people, but in the Divine Right of the rightful King, to whom passive obedience was therefore due. This group of their successors, led by the equally remarkable Bishop Thomas Deacon of Manchester, called itself 'The Catholic Church in England'. By 'Catholic' they meant their own view of the Christian doctrine, worship, and discipline of the united Church of the first three Christian centuries. They sometimes called themselves 'The Orthodox British Church': 'British', because they were also represented in Scotland: 'Orthodox', because in the first three centuries the Church had not separated into West and East, and they had strong affinities with the Eastern Orthodox Church, which still cherishes that same period. They violently disagreed with Rome. They had their differences with the East, but, in some ways, in them West and East did meet.

We will describe their special views when we show their particular influences on the Wesleys. Here we claim that the influence of this High Church group on the Wesleys was wider, deeper, and more lasting than even yet has been recognized. We also claim that because of their special 'Catholic' conception of the unity of the Church, and because the Wesleys wrestled both with this and with the possibilities of wider comprehension in the coming Church, this study has timely significance for more than Anglicans and Methodists, in view of the widespread modern movements towards union.

HOLINESS IN 'HOLY' ORDERS. The distinctive 'Catholic' influence of the Catholic Non-Jurors on Wesley did not begin until 1732. From 1725 onwards, in preparation for his ordinations, Wesley read books about Church of England orders and worship which were broad and tolerant rather than High Church. He also read many books that pleaded for holiness, like those of à Kempis and Taylor, and the many writers of his own Church covered the broad spectrum of Anglican views. His decision, in 1726, to attend communion weekly probably expressed the loyalty of the new Fellow of Lincoln College, Oxford, to University rules and to the Prayer Book rubric about Cathedral and Collegiate Churches. Although his monthly fast on Wednesdays from December 1725 onwards pointed in a High Church direction, there is no convincing proof that he held High Church views of orders or the sacraments. His chief concern was to be holy in *holy* orders.

HOLINESS—OR UNIVERSAL LOVE—IN THE HOME. In 1726 Wesley preached on 'Universal Love' in general defence of his sister Hetty, who had been disowned by his father for serious indiscretions with a lover. He found inspiration for his own sermon in sermons by men of widely different views. The first was Atterbury, a High Churchman, and the second was Samuel Clarke, who was of unorthodox Arian outlook in respect to the person of Christ. The title of Clarke's sermon included the words 'Universal Love' which was to fire Wesley with warm ethical, evangelical, and ecumenical purposes. Wesley expressed the holiness of universal love in family life before it overflowed into the world through the whole family of God.

HOLINESS IN THE FIRST METHODIST SOCIETY. When the Holy Club was founded in 1729, there was still no indication of markedly High Church views. Weekly communion continued. But the idea of holiness was now amplified from a significant source that shaped his future. Wesley first read Law's *Christian Perfection* in 1728, and this gave him the name for his major doctrine of Holiness, i.e. Christian Perfection, and with Law's other book, *A Serious Call*, read in 1730, made him determine afresh to be all-devoted to God. Wesley seized the idea that holiness is not only for men in holy orders, but also for all men, and that its finest feature is universal love.

CHURCH UNITY. In 1731 Wesley read two opposed books about Church unity. *The Life of Bishop Bull* tells of High Church and Non-Juror attempts to bring German Protestantism and the Church of England into full communion on the basis of Episcopacy and the Church of England Liturgy. In contrast, *The Life of Archbishop Ussher* tells of his plan of 1641 for settling the divisions of Christians in this country by a Comprehension Scheme for a modified Episcopacy. This appealed to Baxter, who gave it prominence in the unsuccessful Presbyterian proposals to Charles II in 1660 after the Restoration, for reconciliation with the Bishops. Plans for union by Catholicity and Comprehension were already competing in Wesley's mind.

William Law was a Non-Juror absorbed by the pursuit of holiness. The Non-Jurors were concerned about Church Union. These two aims led Wesley into the next stage of his unfolding experience.

I   THE INFLUENCE OF 'THE CATHOLIC CHURCH IN ENGLAND' ON THE WESLEYS

In 1947 I pointed out in the *London Quarterly Review* that the Manchester Non-Jurors led the Wesleys to practise certain Usages in the Communion Service. This has been amplified by J. C. Bowmer, J. R. Parris, and Trevor Dearing. It is now timely to show that this was a subsidiary part of their influence on his conception of the unity of the Catholic Church.

A week before he landed at Deal on his return from Georgia, in January 1738, Wesley summarized his religious experience in an important private paper which he never published. He paid a tribute to Bishops Taylor and Beveridge, and Mr Nelson but says: 'Only when they interpreted Scripture in different ways I was often much at a loss. And again, there was one thing much insisted on in Scripture—the unity of the Church—which none of them, I thought, clearly explained or strongly inculcated. But it was not long before Providence brought me to those who showed me a sure rule of interpreting Scripture, viz., "Consensus veterum: quod ab omnibus, quod ubique, quod semper creditum". At the same time, they sufficiently insisted upon a due regard to the one Church at all times and in all places' (Journal, i, p. 419).

This rule was the Vincentian Canon, contained in Vincent of Lerins's 'Commonitorium', written A.D. 434, which Wesley read in 1733 and 1734. Vincent says: 'In the Catholic Church itself we take the greatest care to hold *that which has been believed everywhere, always and by all*'. We must 'follow universality, antiquity, and consent'. This claims that if we follow 'universality', i.e. the testimony of the bishops and fathers of the different countries of 'antiquity', i.e. the first three or four centuries, where they agree, i.e. 'consent', we shall be following the guidance of the apostles, and, as Wesley put it, be rightly interpreting Scripture. Wesley also said his new friends 'insisted upon a due regard to the one Church at all times, and in all places', i.e. they also respected the common testimony of the Church in later centuries, including their own. Who were his new friends?

Wesley always believed, as he said above of these new friends, that Providence introduced him to Clayton on 20 April 1732. Clayton helped him to prepare his *Collection of Prayers* published in the following year. In the Preface, Wesley shows he had followed Vincent's rule in preparing it. He says that in his interpretation of the Scriptures, he had 'kept close to that sense of them which the Catholic Fathers and ancient Bishops have delivered to succeeding generations', and his frequent prayers for the unity of the Church of his day were shaped by contact with his new, Providentially selected friends.

Clayton was a scholarly Oxford student, who, after April 1732, worked for over twelve months very closely with the Wesleys in the Holy Club, and they corresponded frequently when Clayton returned to Manchester to become chaplain to the collegiate church. The friendship was not broken until after Wesley's irregular acts, following his conversion. Wesley visited Manchester in 1733 and 1738, and met a group of Anglican Non-Jurors including the famous John Byrom, composer of 'Christians, Awake', and also the distinguished, daring, and scholarly

13

Thomas Deacon, Bishop from 1733 of 'The British Catholic Church', with his own church in Fennell Street.

The Four Usages

The earliest Non-Jurors, best described in Kettlewell's *Life*, read by Wesley in 1732, refused to take the oaths to William in 1689, and were replaced. Some returned to the Church of England when Anne became Queen, which also reconciled Wesley's mother to his father on the same issue, and led to the birth of John!

Another section organized itself into a separate Church. Their leader, Bishop Hickes, in his book *On Schism*, declared the usurping bishops and clergy were in schism from them—'The Catholic Church in England'. On his death in 1715 the Usages Controversy split them. These Usages were in Edward VI's First Prayer Book of 1549,[1] but were not included in the 1662 Book which is still in use. The Usagers separated from those Non-Jurors who preferred the 1662 Book, and produced their Liturgy of 1718, which restored the Usages. 'The Main of the composition' came from the energetic Thomas Deacon. Their Church claimed Apostolic Succession, and had become a Free Church. It is now dead—perhaps a warning. But their influence can be seen in the Alternative Order of Holy Communion in the Church of England

[1] *Prayer-books.* There will be frequent references to certain prayer books so that a brief note will be valuable to the general reader. The 1549 Prayer Book, sometimes called Edward VI's First Prayer Book. This retained much from the earlier Catholic forms. Edward VI's Second Prayer Book of 1552 was more Protestant and was modified under Elizabeth in 1558. All three books contributed to the 1662 Prayer Book which is still in use and has its own additions.

The 1718 Non-Jurors' Liturgy was drawn up by those Non-Jurors who wished to include the Four Usages.

Deacon's 1734 'Compleat Devotions' by Bishop Deacon, contains 'The Publick Offices of the Church', taken from 'The Apostolical Constitutions', the Ancient Liturgies, and the Church of England Common Prayer Book of 1662.

1928 Prayer Book—perhaps a cheering thought. That book contains the four Usages.

1. THE MIXTURE. They mixed water with wine in the Eucharist, as Early Fathers had used it as a reminder of the water and blood which flowed from the side of the Crucified. The cup was a double reminder of cleansing, both by the blood of Christ and by the waters of baptism.

2. MAKING AN OBLATION OF THE ELEMENTS. The 1549, 1718, and 1734 Prayer Books which contain the Usages have the remaining three Usages in the Consecration Prayer, just before the distribution of the Elements. The 1549 Book prays: 'We Thy humble servants do celebrate, and make here before Thy divine Majesty, with these Thy holy gifts, the memorial which Thy Son hath willed us to make.' In what sense did the Wesleys think of this as a sacrifice? And, can we?

3. THE INVOCATION, OR EPICLESIS in the 1549 Book asks: 'with Thy Holy Spirit and word, vouchsafe to bless and sanctify these Thy gifts, and creatures of bread and wine, that they may be unto us the body and blood of Thy most dearly beloved Son, Jesus Christ'. Is God able to use a meal, and our money, more effectively if we ask a 'blessing', but not this Supper?

4. PRAYER FOR THE FAITHFUL DEPARTED is included in the same Consecration Prayer, with no provision for petitions for particular servants of God.

The 1662 Book cut out the Mixture, the Invocation, and part of the Oblation, from the 1549 Communion. The remaining phrase of the Oblation, including 'accept this our sacrifice of praise . . .' was included as an optional prayer after the Administration, where it no longer referred obviously to the Elements. The Prayer for the Dead became a thanksgiving, and was moved to an earlier position. Here we notice two features of the Usagers' 1718 Liturgy. It restored the Usages, but with

the Invocation after the Oblation, a reversal of the 1549
Order. Second, to those familiar with the 1662 Book, the
new position of prayers would seem like 'inverting the
order and method of the Liturgy', a phrase to which we
shall refer later.

Wesley favoured the Usages, clearly under Clayton's
influence, from, at latest, September 1732 onwards.
From October onwards he attended communion at
Christ Church, not his own college, and counted it a
triumph when he persuaded others to do the same,
because the Mixture was constantly used there. His
sermon on 'The Duty of Constant Communion', made in
September 1732, is also evidence for 1787–8, when it was
published. It speaks of 'the Altar' and 'the Christian
Sacrifice'. The Oblation was also the inspiration of much
of his reading in 1732—*The Propitiatory Oblation in the
Holy Eucharist* by J. Johnson, a theologian who greatly
influenced the Non-Jurors' Liturgy of 1718: Brevint's
The Christian Sacrament and Sacrifice, which Wesley
published later and which inspired the Wesleys' *Sacramental Hymns* of 1745: and *Sacrifice the Divine Service*
by J. Scandrett, Non-Juror Vicar of Madeley. As to the
Invocation, in the same sermon Wesley said that by 'a
plain command of Christ . . . the Apostles were obliged to
bless, break and give bread . . .'. 'Bless' is in the account
of the Lord's Supper in the Communion of the 1549 Book,
linked with the Invocation. Wesley's *Notes on the New
Testament* (1754) on 1 Corinthians 10:15, explain 'bless'
as meaning 'setting the cup apart to a sacred use, and
solemnly invoking the blessing of God upon it'. Finally,
in Wesley's *Prayers* of 1733 he ends with a general prayer
for the faithful dead—'O Lord, thou God of spirits and
all flesh, be mindful of Thy faithful, from Abel the just
even to this day. And for Thy Son's sake give to them and
us, in Thy due time, a happy resurrection, and a glorious

rest at Thy right hand for evermore!' The book contains other similar general prayers for the faithful dead.

The evidence shows that the Manchester Non-Jurors had led Wesley to desire the Four Usages, of which only the Mixture was regularly available in Oxford. The dominant influence seems to have been 'The Catholic Church in England', and especially Deacon, who became Bishop of that Church in 1733.

II   THE UNITY OF THE CHURCH AND APOSTOLIC SUCCESSION

The Usages were secondary to unity for Wesley. How did the Manchester Non-Jurors 'clearly explain and strongly inculcate' the unity of the Catholic Church? We have seen that the reading of *The Life of Bishop Bull* in 1730, and *The Life of Archbishop Ussher* in 1731, had set the problem before Wesley without settling it (see p. 11). Could a high form of Episcopacy or a Comprehension Scheme for a modified Episcopacy, unify Protestantism in this country and with German Protestantism?

For Wesley the problem of unity was now as wide as Christianity. Almost daily in his *Prayers* of 1733, there are petitions to God to heal the divisions of 'Thy holy Catholic Church'. There are also frequent prayers for 'the clergy thereof . . . Bishops, Priests, and Deacons', with the implication that there are no other valid ministries within the Catholic Church.

We are therefore not surprised that it is the Episcopal Church for which he prays as 'that branch of Thy Holy Catholic Church which Thou hast planted in these kingdoms'. Unity would come when God would 'give to all heretics humility and grace to make amends to Thy Church'. It is in the light of this that we must estimate Wesley's well-chosen reading about Dissent and the

Church of England in 1732–3. 1732 was an important year in his reading, for it marked the practical disappearance for a time of his general reading and a vast increase in his religious reading.

This Branch Theory of the Catholic Church came originally from Anglican theologians of the time of Charles I. The Non-Jurors also restricted the legitimate branches to Churches in the Apostolic Succession. Wesley read Deacon's *The Doctrine of the Church of Rome Concerning Purgatory* in 1733, in which he says Rome is 'a large unorthodox schismatical *branch* of the universal Church' (ibid p. 140). This was obviously Wesley's view at this time. In 1732–3 he read a number of writings by leading Dissenters, but many more by Church of England writers who took a strong line against Dissent.

He read books by Spurstow, Baxter, and Calamy, leading Presbyterians, by Fox, the founder of the Quakers, and another, defending the Baptists, by John Stennett, one of their leaders. All these books were by leading figures in the Dissenting Churches. Only Spurstow's book is named; it was his devotional book *Meditations*. It may therefore be that at the very time when he was reading Episcopalian attacks, unchurching them, Wesley was admiring the piety of some of these fine Dissenters!

Unchurch them he certainly did. He read a book *On Schism* by John Norris the Cambridge Platonist, who, as a decided Churchman, opposed Nonconformists, saying they were in schism. In his 1733 *Prayers*, Wesley often prays that the Church might, for instance, be defended 'from all the assaults of schism'. He also read *Against the Dissenters*, a book by Bishop King of Derry, a milder appeal to Presbyterians. In 1733 he read *Theologica Comparativa* by James Garden, a strong attack on the scholastic dogmatics of Scottish Presbyterians. Other writers whom he read at this time, for devotional reasons, held high views of orders. John Scott (1639–96) attacked both Dissent and the Roman communion. Bishop S. Patrick (1626–1707), having taken Presbyterian orders, was later episcopally ordained, believing this to be necessary. Wesley read a devotional book 'with prayers before and after sacrament' by Bishop Duppa (1588–1662), who was with Charles I until his execution, greatly influenced Charles II, and believed episcopal government to be of the essence of the Church.

It was in his attitude to the Roman Church that his high claims for the 'branch of the Holy Catholic Church . . . planted in these kingdoms' was stressed in his reading. The phrase itself, of course, meant that he believed the Presbyterians in Scotland, as well as English Dissent, formed no part of the Catholic Church. When, in 1733, he prays of the Catholic Church such prayers as 'where it is *corrupt*, purge it; where it is in error, rectify it', it seems likely he had particularly in mind all polemics he had read against Rome, but three books in particular. In 1733 he had read Deacon's book against the Roman Catholic belief in Purgatory. In 1732 he had read, first, the account of the sufferings of the Lutherans persecuted under the Roman Catholic Archbishop of Salzburg in that very year; second, 'Bishop Bull against Bossuet'. The Anglican Bishop Bull (1634–1710) had written in 1694 asserting the necessity of faith in the divinity of the Son of God for all who would share in catholic communion. Robert Nelson, the Non-Juror, sent a copy of this book to Bossuet, the French Roman Catholic bishop, who congratulated Bull on behalf of the clergy of France but asked what he meant by 'Catholic', and why he remained separate from Rome. Bull replied in *The Corruptions of the Church of Rome*, which would be the book that Wesley read. He appealed to 'the Catholic Church of the first three centuries' as representative of 'the universal Church of Christ of all ages'. (*Judicium Ecclesias Catholicae*, p. xiii.) Christians must continue to 'cleave to that doctrine and faith which was preached with one mouth, as it were, by the Bishops and presbyters in the Apostolic Churches throughout the world, in agreement with the Holy Scriptures'. (Ibid p. 129.) The English Reformation had been faithful to the first three centuries, but Rome had wandered into its corruptions. Armed by this apologetic, Wesley was able later to read the *Life of Bellarmine*, the greatest controversialist for Rome in the early seventeenth century. Late in 1733 he read *A Defence of the Validity of the English Ordinations*, written in 1723 by Fr Courayer, a former Roman Catholic professor.

Wesley criticized his own Church. In his *Prayers* on Thursday morning he prayed the Catholic Church might '*preserve* that doctrine and discipline which thou hast delivered to her', but on Saturday morning he prayed '*restore* to her her ancient discipline'. Wesley says 'ancient discipline'. The sixth proposal of the Non-Jurors in their approach to the Eastern Orthodox Church for a Concordat, from 1716 onwards, was for 'the revival of the ancient godly discipline'. The first book on the 'ancient Church', which Wesley read in 1732, almost certainly after meeting Clayton, was Cave's *Primitive Christianity*, which treats, among other things, of the discipline and penance of the Primitive Church. It is interesting to note that Simon claimed that the original Methodist Rules, those of the United Societies of 1742–3, were based on this book. In 1734 Wesley read Nathaniel Marshall's *The Penitential Discipline of the Primitive Church*. In August 1735, Emily Wesley wrote to him saying she would never put her conscience under the direction, or tyranny, of any frail mortal. It was therefore penitential discipline he had in mind; and its anaemic expression in his own Church. Marshall strongly defended the Church of England against Non-Juror attacks in respect to schism, heresy, perjury, and treason, so the penitential discipline was by no means a monopoly of the Non-Jurors. Indeed, Baxter, the Presbyterian, fought for the rights of the pastor to discipline his members. But the impelling motives which led Wesley to desire a restoration of primitive discipline were derived from his Non-Juror friends.

As Wesley held the Branch Theory of the Catholic Church in 1733, what practical scheme of union did he have in mind when he prayed in his *Prayers* of that year that God would heal its divisions?

Union was discussed hopefully in England during the years say 1710—25, i.e. from Wesley's first communion until his ordination as deacon. Non-Jurors played an important part in these discussions.

a *Union and German Lutheranism*

On the Branch Theory, the Lutherans of Hanover could only qualify as Catholic by first taking Episcopacy into their system. We must remember this was to many an important issue, for Hanover was the other kingdom of the Hanoverian kings of England from 1727 until the accession of Victoria in 1837, and Prussia, as another largely Lutheran kingdom, was also involved. It was in *The Life of Bishop Bull* that Wesley read in 1730 of the attempt to bring German and English Protestantism closer together. In this he would read of the part played in these negotiations by the Non-Juror, Dr J. E. Grabe. Wesley read his *Spicilegium SS. Patrum . . .* in 1725. He was Prussian by birth, and was attracted to the Roman Church by his study of the Fathers in 1695, but Philip Spener, the German Lutheran Pietist, encouraged him to visit Oxford before approaching Rome, and he was ordained here by the Non-Juror Bishop Lloyd, as deacon in 1700, and later as priest.

Frederick I of Prussia wished to unite the two German Protestant Churches, the Lutheran and the Reformed. Partly on the advice of Dr Daniel E. Jablonski, his chaplain, he had the English Liturgy translated, seriously considering using it in his own chapel and the cathedral church. (Here is another fascinating association with Wesley. Jablonski was both Bishop of the Bohemian Church in Poland, and Superintendent of the Bohemian Brethren elsewhere, including the Moravians of Herrnhut. In 1735 he consecrated David Nitschmann in Herrnhut as Bishop of the Moravians. This meant that the Moravian Church at Herrnhut, being episcopal, became independent of the Lutheran Church and acceptable to Wesley, who, in February 1736, saw Nitschmann consecrate Seifart and was greatly impressed.)

Archbishop Sharp of York, greatly admired by Wesley's parents, found the Non-Juror Grabe useful in all these negotiations. R. Nelson's *The Life of Bishop Bull* says that by Grabe's plan to introduce Episcopacy and the English Liturgy into Prussia and Hanover 'he would have united the two main bodies of Protestants, in a more perfect and Apostolical Reformation than that upon which either of them did yet stand' (p. 403). Now Grabe preferred to celebrate communion after the Order of the Scottish Prayer Book of 1637 or the English Liturgy of 1549, and would not attend the 1662 Liturgy. This meant he favoured the Four Usages, including the Invocation of the Holy Spirit, a practice favoured by the Lutherans. It is significant that at about the time Wesley would be completing his 1733 *Prayers* he read three works by Franck, the German Lutheran Pietist. In doing so he was pursuing his double interest in unity and holiness, but, as we shall see later, he was opening a door upon what was, in a sense, a new world of *faith*. These negotiations of 1710–11 came to nothing, but this attempt to promote the unity of the Church evidently stirred Wesley's imagination.

b *Union and Gallican Catholicism*

Between 1717 and 1719 Archbishop Wake of Canterbury corresponded with Dr Du Pin of the Sorbonne. He felt that a Catholic communion of all true Churches of Christ ought to have been possible on the basis of the three Creeds, and piety and charity. He hoped to bring the French theologians to acknowledge the non-episcopal churches as true Churches of Christ, and see them 'break off from the Court of Rome'. (See *The Quest for Catholicity*, G. H. Tavard, p. 116.)

On the other hand, the Non-Jurors were as violent in their rejection of Papal claims and other aspects of the Roman Church as the Archbishop, but Episcopacy was essential to them, and clearly Wesley agreed with them at this time. New possibilities of drawing the Gallican Church towards the Church of England were created when the Papal Bull Unigenitus was made a law of the land by the French King in 1730. It is significant that Wesley studied this Bull in 1733, and his previous reading seems to have been guided by this development. By this act, Louis XIV hoped to scatter the remnants of Jansenism. In 1732 Wesley read Perier's *Life of Pascal*, who was converted to Jansenism in 1646, and who effectively attacked the Jesuits. From 1730 onwards the Jansenists lined up with the Gallicans against ultramontane Romanists, led by the Jesuits, and, politically, the Parliament of Paris was with the Gallicans, and the King with the Ultramontanists. Earlier, in 1732, Wesley had read *On Contentment* by Pierre du Moulin, a prominent Huguenot. In 1733, just before he read the Bull Unigenitus, Wesley

23

studied two books by Fénelon (1651–1715). In view of all this interest in important leaders of the Gallican and Huguenot Churches we can assume that his reading of Bull's reply to Bossuct, another great Gallican leader, on *The Corruptions of the Church of Rome*, would also be inspired by interest in English Protestant courtship of the Gallican Church.

c *Union and the Orthodox Church*

Here again, Non-Jurors took the initiative. From 1716, Collier, Spinckes, Brett and others contacted 'the Catholick and Apostolick Oriental Church' proposing a Concordat. They indicated a dozen points of agreement, and five of disagreement, but the belated reply revealed there were other difficulties. The Patriarchs sent an exposition of faith by the Synod of Jerusalem of 1672. Archbishop Wake intervened in 1725, and correspondence with Constantinople ended. The Non-Juror bishops had also communicated with the 'Holy Governing Synod of Russia', and this was more promising, but the death of Peter the Great, who had been interested, brought this to an end also in 1725. In view of Wesley's obvious interest, we specially note that in 1734 he read *Confessio Ecclesiae Orientalis*. We must not forget his interest in the Orthodox Church, based in the first place on practices common to them and 'The British Orthodox Church' because of their common acceptance of so much in the Apostolical Constitutions and of the Primitive Church.

As the Non-Jurors inspired Wesley in his study of the possibilities of the union of German Lutheranism, Gallican Catholicism, and the Eastern Orthodox Church, they were his guides not only about Vincent's rule for the interpretation of Scripture, but also because 'they sufficiently insisted upon a due regard to the one Church at all times, and in all places'.

III THE UNITY OF THE CATHOLIC CHURCH AND HOLINESS

We have seen that holiness inspired Wesley as he took *holy* orders in the Church of England, and in his leadership of the *Holy* Club. We shall now see that he was still inspired by holiness in his desire for the unity of 'the *Holy* Catholic Church', a title frequently used in the 1733 *Prayers*.

Wesley's re-reading of Law's *Christian Perfection* early in 1732 is reflected in his sermon of 1 January 1733, on 'The Circumcision of the Heart' (II. 8), in his emphasis on self-denial. In the Preface to his *Prayers* (1733) this was linked with mortification, the subject for special meditation on Wednesday and Friday evening. In both sermon and prayers Wesley was therefore supporting the practice of fasting on the Stations, Wednesday and Friday.

In the sermon, humility is emphasized perhaps more than faith, hope, and love. The sermon was probably influenced here again by Law. Wesley followed the sermon by reading Alonso Rodriguez's *Treatise on Humilitie*, which was the particular virtue for meditation on Tuesday evening in the *Prayers*. The method of meditating on a certain virtue at a certain time he also probably derived from Law's same book *A Serious Call*, but Law allocates humility not to a day, but to 9 a.m. daily; people are advised to pray for special objects at 9 a.m., noon, 3 p.m., and 6 p.m. It seems very likely that it was at this time that the Oxford Methodists devised a 'Scheme of Self Examination', which included 'Have I used a Collect at nine, twelve and three? . . . Have I duly meditated? . . . From six, etc. to prayers?' This may also have derived from Law. But another book which Wesley read in 1732, probably under the same Non-Juror influence, although it was one of his mother's favourites, was *The Spiritual Conflict*, by the Italian Roman Catholic, Lorenzo Scupoli, which also advocates aiming at special virtues for definite periods, and has some stress on mortification. At the end of Wesley's sermon on 'The Circumcision of the Heart', he ends this plea for holiness by urging that God 'reign without a rival within'. He supports the plea by quoting 'those children of God . . . who being dead, still speak to us'. Some quotations are closely paralleled in Castaniza, and others seem reminiscent of Taylor, Lucas, Norris, Francis de Sales, and De Renty, whom he had also read.

It is timely to consider here the significance of the influence on Wesley of what M. Schmidt in his *John Wesley* calls Romanic mysticism, and Jean Orcibal in *A History of the Methodist Church in Great Britain* calls Continental Spirituality. Both, but the latter more particularly, pay a tribute to the influence of P. Poiret, a former Huguenot pastor, who did a great deal to popularize spiritual writers of this kind. Orcibal traces to him eleven of the seventeen works by writers of this outlook which Wesley abridged and published, and claims that Wesley was originally introduced to Poiret by John Byrom, who belonged to the Manchester group of Non-Jurors. But Deacon was also well acquainted with Gallican writers, and in August 1732 we find Clayton writing to Wesley of Malebranche and Madame Bourignon, so that these writings were familiar to all the Manchester Non-Jurors.

We therefore notice that in his study of these writers a double interest fused in Wesley's mind. This reading included also Scougal's *Life of God in the Soul of Man*, which Wesley read repeatedly, and for the first time in 1734. Thus he included the spirituality of England and Scotland, France and Germany. His interest was his twin concern for unity and holiness.

M. Schmidt has written in *The History of the Ecumenical Movement* on 'The Ecumenical Movement in Continental Europe during the Seventeenth and Eighteenth Centuries'. He claims that Romanic mysticism was the spiritual bond of unity in Europe in these centuries. Wesley certainly seems to have been aware that this ought to be so, that holiness ought to produce unity.

We have seen that Wesley shows in the Preface to his *Prayers* of 1733 that he accepted the Vincentian rule in the interpretation of Holy Scriptures 'by keeping close to that sense of them which the Catholic Fathers and ancient Bishops have delivered to succeeding generations'. We have also seen that the *Prayers* are inspired by the desire for the unity of the Catholic Church. The Preface goes on to say that the Vincentian Canon helps us to see the five heads of the whole system of Christian Duty. These are: 1. Renouncing ourselves: 2. Devoting ourselves to God: 3. Self-denial: 4. Mortification: 5. 'Christ liveth in me . . . the last stage of christian holiness: This maketh the Man of God perfect: He . . . has given God his whole heart . . . (and) burns with Love to all Mankind.' This, then, was the whole system of Christian Duty, or holiness, delivered by the Catholic Fathers and Ancient Bishops to succeeding generations.

His exploration of the spirituality of Britain, France, and Germany reveals that this was also the ideal of many Christians 'of the whole Church . . . in all places' in the sixteenth, seventeenth, and eighteenth centuries on which he concentrated. This is because the Catholic Church exists to be holy, and therefore to produce holiness. He frequently prays that bishops, priests, and deacons might be blessed with 'apostolic graces'. The discipline of the Church would help to keep her or make her holy, and the source of this holiness is in love. It originates in the love of God, which is the absorbing theme for Sunday, and it is expressed in love of our neighbour, which is very appropriately the virtue on which prayer concentrates at the beginning of the week on Monday. We notice again—as reminded in the Preface—that this is universal love, love for all mankind. So unity and catholicity and apostolicity are aspects of the Church which assist her in producing holiness, or, as Wesley so finely puts it in a phrase in a prayer on Sunday, the day of the love of God, '. . . thy Church is the Catholic seminary of divine love'. The Catholic Church ought unitedly to pursue and to produce Christian perfection, that holiness which is perfect love to God, and universal love of mankind.

CHAPTER TWO

The Apostolical Constitutions,
the Branch Churches, Bishop Deacon, and
'Catholick Union'

1733–1736

LET us first sketch the scheme for unity Wesley would have favoured in 1733. Only one branch of the Catholic Church ought to exist in each country, acting under the divinely commissioned threefold ministry, derived from the apostles by succession through the bishops. Therefore Dissenters ought to return to the Church of England. Rome would need to be purged from her corruptions, the German Protestant State Churches required Episcopacy, and his own Church ought to have a stricter discipline. The Church of England Liturgy, but including the Usages, could draw her closer to the other branches of the Church, particularly the Orthodox Church. Holiness, sacrificially exemplified in the Catholic Church of the first three centuries, and surviving in the Catholic Church of the three centuries from before the Reformation to his own day, must both promote and inspire Church unity.

In the unpublished private paper which has guided us so far, (Journal i, pp. 418–20), Wesley says he next bent the bow too far the other way, 'by making antiquity a co-ordinate rather than subordinate rule with Scripture' and 'by admitting several doubtful writings as undoubted evidence of antiquity'. This period therefore began in 1733, and it ended with Wesley's re-assessment of these writings, the Apostolical Constitutions and Canons, in September 1736.

In 1734 Bishop Deacon of 'The Catholic Church in England' published his *Compleat Devotions*, a version of the Book of Common Prayer of the Church of England greatly revised and supplemented from the Apostolical Constitutions. Wesley was identified with it in that Deacon consulted him about his order for the Psalter, and included at the back of the book extracts from Wesley's 'Essay on the Stationary Fasts'. It has influenced liturgical developments in Scotland, America and our own country. In the Preface Deacon commended it as based on two principles:

1. All Churches should follow 'the *doctrines*, *practices*, *worship* and *discipline*' of the Ancient, Universal Church, from its beginning to the end of the fourth century, as certainly having apostolic authority.

2. The most ancient Christian Liturgy (or Order of Holy Communion), is that in the Apostolical Constitutions, which contains the doctrines and laws believed and obeyed by all in the purest ages, the first three centuries, as derived from apostolic men, and therefore that book ought to be allowed its due authority still.

If these two principles were put into practice, 'a truly Catholick Union would be restored among all Christian churches'.

These 'doubtful writings', the Apostolical Constitutions, contain some fascinating pictures of the Church of the first three centuries—and later.[1] At Oxford in about

[1] Books I-VI of the *Apostolical Constitutions*, based on the Didascalia, probably originated in Syria midway through the third century. Book VII amplifies the Didache, undiscovered in Wesley's day, and dated by some A.D. 80–100, and by others 120–160. Book VIII, from which the 1718 Non-Juror Liturgy derived the Usages, was probably

September 1734 Wesley studied Whiston's *Primitive Christianity Revived* (1711), which contains this book in Greek and English, and the eighty-five Apostolic Canons which end it. Whiston believed its laws were delivered by Christ to the Apostles after the Resurrection! He says, 'I must own, as to myself, that I cannot read them without the same regard I pay to any Book of the Bible ... nor disobey the Duties therein delivered' any more than those in the 'uncontested Books of the New Testament', (vol. 3, pp. 11–12). The scholarly Non-Jurors, Brett and Hickes, also gave high authority to this book, and particularly to its Liturgy. In September 1734 Wesley thought the Stationary fasts, ordered in Canon 69, to be 'very ancient, if not apostolic', (Letters i, 183). In 1735–6 he seems to have felt bound by Canon 27 (Whiston's numbering), which says clergy who were ordained deacons when unmarried, must remain celibate—still a rule of the Orthodox Church—for, perhaps whimsically, he thought it would be an advantage that when he began missionary work among the Indians, the women would be 'almost a different species'! (Ibid., p. 189.)

I   THE APOSTOLICAL CONSTITUTIONS, AND UNITY
     OF THE BRANCHES OF THE CATHOLIC CHURCH

Our argument is that in Georgia Wesley went beyond the Usagers like Hickes and Brett, and introduced many practices in worship and discipline from the Apostolical Constitutions, mainly in agreement with Deacon. This acceptance of Deacon's two principles was inspired by a

drawn mainly from the 'Egyptian Church Order', and this in turn from the 'Canons of Hippolytus' of about A.D. 220. Deacon followed far more of its precedents than the Usages, in his *Compleat Devotions* of 1734. Although the book has elements from even later than A.D. 500, many parts are very ancient.

desire to restore 'a truly Catholick Union' of the branches of the Catholic Church.

Wesley's innovations in Georgia were inspired by a real admiration for the Primitive Church. The modern Church could learn by comparing its own failures with the achievements of that Church—the work of its varied lay ministries and the witness of its martyrs, its conversion and instruction of pagans, and its speedy winning of political recognition and religious leadership throughout the Empire. Wesley would also see the practical value for unity, of the acceptance of new life from the undivided Church of the first three centuries. In the book *We Belong To One Another*, various writers point out modern affinities between the Orthodox Church and Methodism. Wesley retained more affinities with the East until the end of his life, than he effectively transmitted to Methodism, but he was never more sympathetic than in the years 1733–6. In 1734 he read 'Confessio Ecclesiae Orientalis', a Confession of the Eastern Orthodox Church. He would know of the acceptance by that Church of eighty-five Apostolic Canons, fifty of which had originally been accepted by Rome. The honest and useful acceptance by his own Church of some of the Apostolical Constitutions and Canons could increase the affinity of the three branches of the Catholic Church. Deacon's two principles seemed to provide a promising route towards 'a truly Catholick Union'.

II   WORSHIP IN THE APOSTOLICAL CONSTITUTIONS, AND UNITY

a *The Liturgy*

The Liturgy in Book VIII is so highly stressed by Deacon that we must consider how far it influenced the Wesleys in Georgia.

The evidence is varied. First there are two fascinating papers, which we will call MS. X and MS. Y, which were Notes made by Wesley in September 1736 about the Apostolical Constitutions and Canons (see Appendix to Chapter Three). In August 1737, certain Grievances against Wesley for his innovations were brought before the Grand Jury in Savannah, and later formulated in Indictments. Finally, in 1741, Dr Tailfer and other landowners, all Georgian opponents of Wesley, published *A True Narrative of the State of Georgia*.

(i) At Oxford, Wesley preferred the Usages; in Georgia, he publicly practised them.

Wesley's Diary for 1 May 1737 includes 'subscribed the prayers', but even if this meant the declaration of adherence to the principles of the Church of England made by an incumbent, which is uncertain, he had been free to experiment for the greater part of his ministry there. On his voyage to Georgia, Wesley read many Non-Juror books, and particularly *Reasons for Restoring the Usages* to the Prayer Book, by Bishop Collier of 'The Catholic Church in England'. In the *London Quarterly and Holborn Review*, (January 1947), I argued that Wesley's Diary entry on 5 March 1736, two days before he began his ministry in Savannah, i.e. 'revised Common Prayer-book', meant he brought it into harmony with the 1549 Prayer Book, in accordance with the ideals of the Non-Jurors. The special Non-Juror influence is revealed in the MS. Y. After a careful study of the Apostolical Constitutions and Canons, Wesley wrote a list of six duties and three prudential practices. He begins the duties, 'I believe *myself* it is a duty to observe, so far as I can *without breaking communion with my own Church*: [in the MS. a line is drawn through the words in italics.]

1. To baptize by immersion.

2. To use Water, Oblation of the Elements, Invocation, Alms, a Prothesis, in the Eucharist.

3. To pray for the Faithful Departed'.

As there would be no danger of excommunication for private practice of the Usages, he meant public Eucharists. The Narrative said he mixed 'wine with water in the sacrament'. Charles Wesley records 'offering up the Christian Sacrifice' in March 1736, which was Deacon's subtitle for the 'Holy Liturgy', and therefore meant the Oblation, just as 'consecrate the sacrament' [Charles Wesley's Journal for 10 April 1736] referred to the Invocation. Therefore he publicly practised the Usages.

The sequence 'Oblation . . . Invocation' reverses the order of these two Usages in the 1549 Prayer Book. The Usagers did this in their 1718 Liturgy, as did Deacon in his 1734 *Compleat Devotions*, because this was the sequence in the Apostolical Constitutions. In a book already quoted, one writer refers to the Sacramental Hymn of the Wesleys of 1745, ('Come, Holy Ghost, Thine influence shed . . .'), in which there is an Invocation. He rightly says that if a Methodist minister inserts this before the Prayer of Humble Access, he turns the 1662 Book into the 1549 Book, but this is neither Wesley's sequence nor that of the Orthodox Church, with which the Non-Jurors agreed. They insisted on the sequence—Account of the Institution, Oblation, and then Invocation. We have already noticed that to those familiar with the 1662 Book, the restoration of the Usages would mean 'inverting the order and method of the Liturgy', one of the accusations brought against Wesley in August 1737. Wesley therefore publicly used the 1662 Book for a time, having restored the Usages from the 1549 Book, but putting them in the order taken by the Non-Jurors from the Apostolical Constitutions.

34

We mention here two differences between Wesley and Deacon. Firstly, although both rejected the Roman Catholic belief in Purgatory, Deacon provided for prayers for individual Christians who had died, (following the Apostolical Constitutions VIII 41), whereas Wesley provided in his 1733 *Prayers* a general prayer for the faithful dead, in harmony with the 1549 and 1718 Prayer Books and the Apostolical Constitutions (VIII 13). This practice he often defended. Secondly, although Wesley had sympathies for the Stuarts, in the 1733 Book he prayed, 'Bless King George', whereas Deacon was an active Jacobite as well as a Non-Juror. There is a pathetic background to this double difference. In 1745, when Prince Charles with his invading Highlanders reached Manchester, Clayton offered prayers in a Salford street for 'the new king'. Bishop Deacon secured support for Charles, and with the blessing of their father, Deacon's three sons fought for the invader. One son was executed in London, and his head was sent to Manchester and put on a pole outside the exchange, near to the head of another rebel member of his father's 'true British Church'. We are told that the father was one of the first to go to see the heads of his son and friend, and raised his hat, and thanked God for their constancy. Doubtless he also prayed for his boy.

(ii) So far, Wesley seems to have followed the 1718 Liturgy slightly more closely than Deacon's 1734 Book, but now we consider some of his preferences and practices which are not found in the other Liturgies, but are in Deacon's 1734 Liturgy, and in which he followed the Apostolical Constitutions.

There is no evidence that Wesley practised infant communion in Georgia, but in 1749 he questioned whether it is an abuse, which indicates how he was thinking in Georgia. 'Infant communion' does not mean administration to 'boys' which Wesley did in 1737 under Moravian inspiration, but administration to infants in arms, a practice common to the Orthodox Church, Deacon, and the Apostolical Constitutions.

On 9 May 1736 Wesley began the practice of having morning service at five, a practice he continued in the days of the Revival. These services were like the cock-crow meetings of the Early Church. Communion with sermon was at eleven, and Wesley withheld the Benediction 'until all the hearers except his own communicants were withdrawn', as the Grievances complained. The dismissal of those 'who are not of the number of the Faithful' and the later Benediction, are found in Deacon, following the Apostolical Constitutions. Wesley felt it right to withhold the blessing from those who rejected the blessing of Communion.

In MS. Y, Wesley felt it a duty to 'use . . . a Prothesis'. Deacon prescribes the use of this side-altar for the preparation by the deacon of the bread and wine, and then the mixing of the water, all to be brought later to the priest to place them 'reverently' on the altar—a procession which survived in Scottish Presbyterianism and in the Orthodox Church. One is reminded of the preparations in the Upper Room.

Finally the Narrative accused Wesley of 'suppressing, in the administration of the Sacrament, the explanation adjoined to the words of communicating by the Church of England to show that they mean a feeding on Christ by faith, saying no more than, "The Body of Christ; the Blood of Christ".' In all the books we have considered, the form nearest to this is in Deacon's book and the Apostolical Constitutions. The words for the bread are identical, but Wesley cut down even their brief formula for the wine, which was 'The Blood of Christ, the cup of life'. We must stress that Wesley followed the Non-Jurors in strongly repudiating transubstantiation.

How trustworthy is this Narrative? Written by Pat Tailfer, Hugh Anderson, D. Douglas, and other Georgian landowners then in Charlestown, South Carolina, it was printed there, and published in 1741, and also sold in Fleet Street, London. The edition issued by the University of Georgia Press in 1960, quotes Moses Coit Tyler as saying, 'As a polemic, it is one of the most expert pieces of writing to be met with in our early literature.' The Narrative repeats most, but not all the charges against Wesley which he reports in his Journal, to which it refers. Where it makes charges not recorded in the Journal, it is credible. For instance, it tells of Wesley 'appointing Deaconesses' which has only recently been fully confirmed by M. Schmidt (see p. 39). It says Wesley used the Mixture, which Wesley confirms in his MS. Y. The authors of the Narrative had no access to these sources of evidence. Consequently as their evidence about Wesley's words of administration harmonizes with the Apostolical Constitutions, unknown to them, there is strong presumption that this evidence is reliable.

Why did Wesley simply say, 'The Blood of Christ'? Thomas Rattray (1684–1743) helped to translate into Greek the proposals of the Non-Juror bishops of England for a Concordat with the Eastern Orthodox Church in 1716. In the Usages Controversy he helped the Scottish bishops, who were also Non-Jurors, to try to heal the breach. Bishop of Dunkeld from 1732, Rattray became Primus of Scotland in 1739. He thought the Liturgy of James was originally that of the Jerusalem Church, which would link us closely with the Upper Room. By comparing it with other Liturgies, and especially with that in the Apostolical Constitutions, he cut out what he considered the interpolations in the Liturgy of James, and believed he had reproduced 'The Ancient Liturgy of the Church at Jerusalem'. Grisbrooke claims that 'not even the passage of two hundred years has completely outmoded' his work. (*Anglican Liturgies of the 17th and 18th Centuries*, vii.)

Rattray's book was published in 1744, and so was not available to Wesley in Georgia. Wesley may have had contacts through the Manchester Non-Jurors with Rattray, but it seems possible that he had anticipated Rattray, for his Words of Administration were identical with those which Rattray argued were in the original Liturgy of the Church at Jerusalem—'The Body of Christ . . . the Blood of Christ'.

The very day I wrote the above, the joint Convocations of the Church of England approved an amended form of a new experimental communion service. It makes it possible to use, or not to use, the Oblation. The Words of Administration are identical with those of Rattray, the very words used by Wesley in Georgia 230 years ago! The words used for the bread would have been recognized more readily by Wesley's converts in Georgia from Rome had they had the 'Community Mass in English' issued by the Roman Catholic Church in England in 1964, for Wesley's words are identical! Perhaps when Wesley explained his positive reasons for rejecting transubstantiation, his converts believed more honestly than they had done before. This was no mere liturgical exercise for Wesley. He deeply loved to meet his Lord in His own appointed way. He searched beyond all the Liturgies we have considered, apparently beyond even the Apostolical Constitutions, believing that in this way our Lord would have His sacramental Body help to unite the Body of His Church.

b *Baptism*

Two days after landing in Georgia, on 8 February 1736, Wesley met the great Moravian leader Spangenberg, who recorded in his diary that Wesley stressed his plan for evangelizing the Indians in the manner of the Early Church. He thought 'there ought . . . to be ordained *deaconesses* to conform to the early Christian practice of baptism by immersion for women. His standard for primitive Christianity was in general the concensus of opinion from the Fathers of the first three centuries.' (M. Schmidt, *John Wesley*, p. 152.) The same desire for propriety inspired ordination for deaconesses in the Apostolical Constitutions. (III 15.) Deaconesses assisted the priest at baptisms for women. Deacon provided a 'Form . . . of . . . Ordaining Deaconesses'. Two centuries after Wesley argued for ordained deaconesses, Methodism had her first authorized form for 'The Ordination of Deaconesses'. He appears to have trained Miss Bovey as lay deaconess. The Narrative condemned Wesley for '*appointing* Deaconesses, with sundry other innovations which he called the Apostolical Constitutions'.

On 22 February 1736 Wesley baptized a child by trine immersion, and Charles did the same on 14 March. Wesley justified immersion as the Church of England rule, and 'the custom of the first Church', but the Diary reveals that he meant trine immersion. He was appealing not to the 1549 Prayer Book where it is prescribed, but to 'the first', i.e. the Early Church, and especially to the Apostolic Canon 50, which stresses the reference to the Trinity. Deacon practised trine immersion and it is stressed in the Orthodox Church.

Three Duties and one Prudential Practice in Wesley's MS. Y are all seen to be expressions of Wesley's interest in baptism, when we interpret them in the light of the

39

association of baptism and resurrection in the Apostolical Constitutions and Deacon's book. Wesley said he believed it a duty, '1. To baptize by immersion', probably meaning trine immersion. Duty 4 was '*To pray standing on Sunday* in Pentecost'. (Deacon makes this a duty for all *days* between Easter and Pentecost, and explains the motive as 'respect to and remembrance of our Saviour's resurrection'. By Pentecost Wesley means the period from Easter to Pentecost.) Duty 5 was 'To observe *Saturday and Sunday* Pentecost as Festival'. All Sundays are generally recognized as Greater Festivals, and Deacon recognized all other *days* in Pentecost as Lesser Festivals. These two duties are related to baptism in that Deacon says 'Public Baptism may be administered on any day between Easter and Pentecost', which is supported by Tertullian (*de Bapt.* 19) but not in the Apostolical Constitutions! Wesley's Prudential Practice 3 was 'To turn to the East for the Creed'. Deacon provides for this in the Liturgy, and also for the adult, before the act of baptism, when he acknowledges his association with Christ in a baptismal Creed. This baptismal practice follows combined precedents in the Apostolical Constitutions VII 41 and 44. The slight differences confirm that, in September 1736, Wesley consulted other authorities about the practices of the Early Church.

The association of baptism and resurrection which makes these four practices meaningful, is well expressed in the baptismal order in the Constitutions. Before the actual baptism, the catechumen makes his baptismal confession, (VII 41). Deacon says he must do this facing the east, thus linking it with the first act of the candidate after baptism, when, as the Constitutions say, he must 'stand up and pray that prayer which the Lord taught us . . . *he who is risen again ought to stand up and pray*, because he that is raised up, stands upright. Let him therefore, who has been dead with Christ, and is raised up with Him, stand up. But let him pray towards the east'. 2 Chronicles 5:12 is quoted to justify this last act. (VII 44.)

The present writer is not inclined to relish symbolic religious acts unduly. The act of standing for the 'offering' can become symbolic of adoration of money. Bishops and people stood to dedicate *themselves* to God through Christ before communicating, (ibid., VIII 13). To stand with others on special occasions, between Easter and Whit Sunday, as a reverent and joyful reminder both of the resurrection of Christ and of our own personal spiritual resurrection, could be an inspiring renewal of dedication.

III   PRACTICES IN THE APOSTOLICAL CONSTITUTIONS
       AND UNITY

Deacon also claimed that practices in the Apostolical Constitutions could promote unity. We have already mentioned some of these practices in relation to the sacraments. On 25 May 1736 Charles Wesley 'read the prayers for the energumens', i.e. the demon-possessed, over a distressed girl of fifteen. Deacon provides 'prayers for energumens' from the Apostolical Constitutions. The Wesleys continued exorcism when they returned from Georgia. Their concern was Christlike, but the Church must develop many specialized modern ministries, including that to the mentally distressed. Wesley continued his fasting on Stationary Days following Deacon and the Apostolical Constitutions, before and after September 1736, when he included it among Prudential Practices.

IV   DISCIPLINE

Wesley's discipline in Georgia was partly based on Church of England rule, but even more upon his high

41

regard for the authority of the Apostolic Ministry. Shortly after arriving in Georgia he said he must have notice under the rubric from those intending to communicate, presumably so that he might warn those he judged not qualified ecclesiastically or morally, not to attend.

a *Authority of Ministry in the Apostolical Succession asserted through Rebaptism*

The Wesleys were familiar with *Lay Baptism Invalid* before going to Georgia. It was written to prove 'such Baptism is Null and Void when administered in opposition to the Divine Right of the Apostolical Succession'. It was based on the Apostolical Canon 68 which said that baptism by heretics was null, and was written by Roger Laurence, who was consecrated with Deacon about 1733, as Bishop of 'The Catholic Church in England'. Wesley rebaptized a German, Charles was ready to rebaptize a Dutchman. Wesley continued this practice in Georgia until at least June 1737, and the Narrative says his rule applied to 'all Dissenters of whatever denomination'.

b *His Penitential System*

The Narrative speaks of Wesley's 'endeavours to reestablish, Confessions, Penance, Mortifications', which with 'other innovations . . . he called Apostolic Constitutions'. Trevor Dearing thinks Wesley was following Deacon and the Apostolical Constitutions, and demanded public confession as a condition for communicating. This is not completely certain, for, although this was one charge in the original Grievances, it was dropped from the Indictments which followed. Deacon provided a 'Form of Admitting to Penance' for use in Sunday Morning Prayer, after 'unbelievers' had been dismissed. The penitent confessed publicly before the priest, in the presence, and presumably in the hearing, of the faithful, and the priest told him what penance the bishop had ordered. A passage in the Apostolic Constitutions (II 39–43) speaks of the confession, but does not make it clear where it was to be made.

Deacon also provided a 'Penitential Office' for the penitents and faithful for use on Wednesdays and Fridays, the Stationary Days. This seems to have influenced Wesley's selection of confessional and penitential hymns for the second part of his Charlestown Hymnbook of 1737, which was for use in his Society, so that it seems very likely that he used something like Deacon's 'Penitential Office' on those days. It is possible the Society formed in 1736 was used for confession, in which case his 'conversing singly with each' would describe the more personal confessions. Whatever the method and conditions, Wesley did attempt to establish discipline through confession, penance and mortification. Wesley did not dismiss unbelievers from Morning Prayer, which was at 5 a.m., but from Communion after the sermon at 11 a.m. We cannot be certain that all the small company who communicated, submitted to the discipline, so that the Narrative was probably apt in speaking of his 'endeavours'. We recognize again the influence of Deacon, and, perhaps even more, of the Apostolical Constitutions.

V CONCLUSION

Deacon claimed that if 'the doctrines, practices, worship and discipline' of the first centuries were followed, particularly as recorded in the Apostolical Constitutions, 'a truly Catholick Union' would be restored. We have seen that Wesley followed the Apostolical Constitutions perhaps more consistently than he did either the 1718 or 1734 Prayer Books of the Usagers. In doing this he had drawn closer to the Orthodox Church, but although this might have had value elsewhere, in Georgia, with its many Dissenters, it was a handicap, apart from his efforts to win Roman Catholics. The Narrative says, 'While all Dissenters . . . were . . . shut out from religious ordinances . . . persons suspected to be Roman Catholics were received by him'. Wesley said that in May 1737 he convinced a number of Roman Catholics of the grievous errors of the Church of Rome, doubtless using ideas derived from Deacon and Bishop Bull, and received them into the Church of England. He may have followed his strong attack on transubstantiation with the use in the Liturgy, on this single occasion, of the Words of Administration so familiar to them—simply, 'The Body of Christ'. There is no mention of rebaptism, but, although he accepted them as from a true but corrupt branch, he had convinced them that they had entered the true branch of the Catholic Church for English America.

At the commencement of this chapter we sketched the scheme of unity Wesley would probably have favoured in 1733. We have seen that between then and September 1736 he had added many things under the stimulus of Deacon's *Compleat Devotions* of 1734, but on what he considered the high, and probably apostolic authority of the Apostolic Constitutions and Canons. We are now to consider what effect Wesley's re-assessment of the authority of these 'doubtful writings' had upon his conception of Catholicity and Unity in September 1736.

CHAPTER THREE

Scripture, The Apostolical Constitutions, German Protestantism, and 'Catholick Union'

1736–1738

I   THE LUTHERAN CHURCHES AND PIETISM

Wesley was greatly influenced by his reading of *Nicodemus, or The Fear of Man*, both at Oxford in 1733–4 and also in Georgia. Probably it led him to question whether he himself was converted, and also dared him to be a missionary. It was written by A. H. Francke, the great German Lutheran Pietist, for whom Wesley had an increasing admiration. The Pietist Missionary challenge had previously come through the account of the work of the Danish mission in South India, read to him when a boy, and which he read about again in 1730 at Oxford.

Direct personal contact came in Georgia when Wesley met the Salzburgers. At Oxford, in 1732–3, he read of the Roman Catholic persecution they had faced. M. Schmidt reveals the strains between them and the Moravians. (*John Wesley*, 169–78.) They emigrated to Georgia under the patronage of Pietist Lutherans of Augsburg and Halle. In spite of his high regard for the holy zeal of the Pietists, Wesley refused communion to Boltzius, the Lutheran pastor of the Salzburgers, on 17 July 1737, claiming these were his instructions, but it is clear that it also represented his own convictions. Boltzius said there was no actual word of the Lord in favour of ordination and succession, and offered to demonstrate from the Early Fathers the very opposite of episcopal authority, (Schmidt, ibid., pp. 179–81), but it is clear that Wesley still stressed his convictions concerning Apostolic Succession and the need for such succession to ensure validity of sacraments. Lutheran State Churches could become branches of the Catholic Church by taking Episcopacy into their system under the Apostolic Succession.

II   THE MORAVIANS, SCRIPTURE, AND CATHOLICITY

a *The Moravians and Unity*

From the commencement of his contacts with the Moravians, Wesley was greatly impressed by their faith and the primitive and indeed apostolic quality of their Church life. On the voyage to America and in Georgia, by word and example they challenged him as to his own personal faith and experience of salvation. He was deeply moved when witnessing the consecration of Bishop Seifart on 28 February 1736, and imagined himself in an assembly presided over by Paul the tent maker, or Peter the fisherman, under the power of the Spirit. He would also think of the Moravians as the spearhead of Episcopacy in Protestant Germany. The Herrnhut Moravians had only taken back their original Episcopacy into their system in the previous year, from the Brethren of Poland. Bishop Nitschmann, who consecrated Seifart, was the first in this renewed line of bishops. Bishop Jablonski, who was over the Poland Brethren, had previously acted as Lutheran Superintendent over the Herrnhut Moravians, before he consecrated Nitschmann. Jablonski had almost persuaded Frederick I of Prussia, their homeland, to introduce the English Liturgy into his royal chapel, and Hanover, George III's other kingdom, could have been affected by the renewal of any such movement towards union.

On 1 February 1737, after having seen the Bishop of London on the same subject, Charles Wesley saw the Bishop of Oxford, and records, 'I . . . told him the Bishop of London had declined having anything to do with Georgia, and said it belonged to the Archbishop only to unite the Moravians with us. He replied it was the Bishop of London's proper office; but bade me assure the Count we should acknowledge the Moravians as our brethren, and one Church with our own.' John Wesley anticipated the Archbishop, for, on 21 September 1736 he administered 'the communion with the Moravians'. He would be able to assure them that his Liturgy, with its inclusion of the Usages, was similar to that commended with some success to Hanoverians and Prussians, at the same time as Jablonski's efforts, by the Non-Juror Grabe, himself a Prussian and influenced, like them, by the Pietists.

b *Wesley's Re-assessment of the Apostolical Constitutions*

The date of the communion with the Moravians is significant. Just over a week before, on 13 September 1736, Wesley began reading Bishop Beveridge's *Pandectae Canonum Conciliorum*, which deals with all Canons attributed to the Apostles, including those in the Apostolical Constitutions, and those of four General and a number of Provincial Councils. He ended this reading on 20 September, the day before the communion, and from then on he read it night after night with the Moravians until 26 September. He then began prolonged study of it in the mornings, finishing it on 4 October. On 5 October he read 'Cotelerius', almost certainly this scholar's *Apostolic Fathers*, which includes the Greek version of the Apostolical Constitutions in the first edition, and also the Latin version, in the second edition. There is evidence that he also had Whiston's edition with him. He was now really testing, by examining these 'doubtful writings' along with Episcopalians of a strongly Lutheran outlook, whether there was any practical possibility of promoting 'a truly Catholick Union' in Deacon's way, by following the Church of the first three centuries as revealed in the Apostolical Constitutions and Canons.

(i) *From October 1736, Wesley clearly accepted the Supremacy of Scripture.* In the footnote, I have summarized the evidence that the MSS. X and Y are notes of Wesley's study and decisions at this time. The account of his conclusions is supplemented here from Journal entries made at the time, and also from the important unpublished paper dated 25 January 1738, which has guided us so well. (Journal i, 274ff; 418–20.) These will be distinguished by the dates 1736 and 1738.

Beveridge's book convinced Wesley 'that both Particular and "General Councils may err and have erred" . . . and that *things ordained by Councils as necessary to salvation have neither strength nor authority unless they are taken out of Holy Scripture*'. (Journal 1736.) The editor of the Journal does not notice that Wesley is quoting Article XXI, but clearly the Moravians had voiced this attitude to Scripture and General Councils. Huss, their spiritual ancestor, had derived it from Wyclif, and transmitted it to Luther. Here, Wesley was moving away from the Roman and Orthodox position, although in more recent years the latter has introduced some qualification in its reverence for General Councils, stressing the need for their decisions to be received and lived by the whole people of God. (*The Orthodox Church*, Ware, 255–7.) We have italicized what is a continuation of Article XXI, although there are no quotation marks, because the stress of things necessary to salvation became a characteristic of Wesley and he may have been quoting from memory or else adapting. Later he urged that 'the Catholic Spirit' ought to inspire all denominations to co-operate in mission to win the country to justification by faith, and holiness.

(ii) *True antiquity is still 'a sure rule of interpreting Scripture'.* On 25 January 1738, shortly before his conversion, Wesley stated afresh the Vincentian rule of Universality, Antiquity, and Consent. (Journal 1738.) Both MSS. X and Y reveal that this canon had guided him in his re-assessment of the Apostolical Constitutions and Canons, so that he no longer accepted them as 'undoubted evidences of antiquity'. (Journal 1738.) He set aside canons that were merely provincial, or had become obsolete by A.D. 300, or were introduced later, and he had a higher respect for what survived the test. Holiness was the supreme depositum, which was passed to this first period from the Lord through the Apostles, which survived into the three centuries which included his own, and which was to be inherited and handed on by the Methodists. Have we been true to the trust?

Those things which survive the Vincentian test from antiquity, provide 'a subordinate' rather than 'a co-ordinate rule . . . with Scripture'. (Journal 1738.) He was still convinced, for instance, that the Usages were Scriptural, and that true antiquity was a reliable guide to the general nature of the Oblation and Invocation, for the Duties in MS. Y were practices for which, Wesley believed (rightly or wrongly) he had the authority of Scripture.

c *He now Stresses the Value of Prudential Practices*

(i) In *A Plain Account of the Methodists* (1748), Wesley describes what he meant by 'prudential'. He defends classes and similar typical Methodist meetings, which he recognizes as temporary, saying, 'We declare them all to be merely prudential; not essential, not of divine institution . . . Scripture, in most points, gives only general rules, and leaves particular circumstances to be adjusted by the common sense of mankind.'

(ii) Wesley's list of Prudential Practices in MS. Y is obviously incomplete. In MS. X he says of Apostolic Canon 69, 'Commanding to keep Lent and the Stations— not extant in Tertullian's time', and on these grounds he includes both practices in the Prudential Practices as not belonging to true antiquity because so late, but he stresses Holy Week because it was observed earlier in history than Lent. He therefore qualifies not only the Apostolical Constitutions, but also the 1662 Prayer Book, which gives 'The Forty Days of Lent' as 'Fast Days which are to be observed'. Similarly, he says of Canon 68, 'The baptism (of) hereticks null—not extant before St Cyprian', who was rather later than Tertullian, but he does not include rebaptism among his Prudential Practices, although he continued to practise it until January 1739 and possibly later, in the first stages of the Revival! (His comment on 'Canon 52. Commanding to receive penitents—not extant before the grand dispute about it', refers again to the time of Cyprian, but it is ambiguous. It may indicate some questioning of discipline by penance.)

Therefore we must ask which Scriptural principle lies behind each Prudential Practice. Behind Lent and the Stations, obviously there is the Scriptural expectation that Christians will fast. Similarly, Wesley held until at least 1746, that the Apostles prescribed Episcopacy and the Succession, and so, even after September 1736, he followed what he considered the common-sense application of this by many in the Early Church, and rebaptized willing Dissenters.

(iii) Whatever we may think of particular Prudential

Practices, this widening of the door of common sense was invaluable. It meant that Wesley was free to meet eighteenth-century needs from his wide knowledge of precedents in the Primitive Church, and also by direct common-sense search for the best solutions.

d *He was still Concerned about Unity*

He had partly reverted to his position of 1733 in that practices he had added since then from the Apostolical Constitutions were now regarded as Prudential. He still believed in Episcopacy and the Apostolic Succession, the Church of England Liturgy, including the Usages, and the Branch Theory of the Catholic Church, for which Lutheranism could qualify by accepting the two former points. It is possible that he stressed spiritual resurrection rather more, in a relation to baptism by immersion which he nowhere defines in this period, but which we assume included Baptismal Regeneration in some sense.

But his 1733 position was now amplified by a stress on the Supremacy of Scripture, and an emphasis on the doctrines of salvation, which was to lead to fuller experience in his 'evangelical conversion' in May 1738.

These six years left permanent elements in his character. From 1732 until 1733 he had been influenced by the more moderate Usagers, Anglican and fully Non-Juror, and from 1734 until September 1736 this influence had been widened by that of Deacon, his special friends of 'The Catholic Church in England', and the Apostolical Constitutions and Canons. All these influences continued from the new adjustment of September 1736 onwards, so that in January 1738 he was still concerned for 'that one thing insisted on in Scripture—the unity of the Church'. He had sought for it through the worship and discipline of the Primitive Church and the pursuit of holiness. He returned from Georgia with a yearning need for saving faith, combined with a deep concern for the unity of the Catholic Church.

Wesley's MSS. X and Y

J. C. Bowmer's excellent *The Lord's Supper in Early Methodism*, (LSEM), gives the fullest account of these. The Rev. G. Herber Davies of Wesley's Chapel, where they are preserved, has kindly supplied additional information.

There is romantic interest in MS. X, in which Wesley noted on the Apostolic Canon 27, 'Forbidding the clergy to marry—not extant before the Council of Nice'. The Orthodox Church still obeys this rule that ordained bachelors must remain unmarried. In September 1736 Wesley discovered the late origin of this Apostolic Canon 27, and his note shows he realized that celibacy was now not a duty for him, but a prudential practice. Soon afterwards he seems to have had thoughts of marriage with a certain young lady. Early in his ministry in Savannah, he said that under the rubric he would expect notice from those intending to communicate. He was defied by a young married woman: he repelled her from communion in August 1737; this led to the Grievances and Indictments; and this young married woman, Mrs Williamson, was Sophy Hopkey, who so nearly became Mrs Wesley!

(a) MS. X. These are *Wesley's notes on the Apostolical Constitutions and Canons*. (LSEM, 236–7.) All three pages are headed '*Apost. Const.*'.

Page 1. (Not included in LSEM.) After three short untraced quotations, Wesley quotes seven Greek words from Book V 15, showing his interest in the Stationary Days which are commanded in this paragraph. There was almost certainly one earlier paper dealing with I–IV.

Page 2. (LSEM, 236.) There are references to nine items from VI 24 onward to VIII 32. On VII 23 Wesley denies that the betrayal took place on Wednesday, the explanation given here for the Wednesday fast, because John 13 says it happened on the Friday.

Page 3. (LSEM 236–7.) This has references to VIII 33 and 42. After a space, there are critical comments on six of the Apostolic Canons. He evidently questions the full authority of five of them on the grounds of their comparatively late appearance in the first three centuries. We place this MS. X before Y on the grounds that his comments on Canon 69, 'Commanding to keep Lent and the Stations —not extant in Tertullian's time', could have provided him with a reason for placing these customs among the Prudential Practices on MS. Y. One comment deals with the Canon concerned with the Celibacy of the Clergy, which Beveridge numbers 26, and Whiston 27.

As Wesley uses 27, he very probably also had Whiston's edition with him.

Page 4 is blank on both MSS.

(b) MS. Y. Notes on Beveridge's book *Pandectae Canonum Conciliorum*, which deals with the Apostolic Canons. (LSEM, 235–6.)

Page 1. There are notes dealing with pages 9–55 of Beveridge's book, which are not in LSEM because they are difficult to decipher.

Page 2 is reproduced in full in LSEM 236, and deals with items from pp. 58–99 of Beveridge's book.

Page 3 has the list of important Duties and Prudential Practices accepted by Wesley as a result of this study. These are used in relevant places in the preceding chapter.

Urlin and Rattenbury claimed X and Y were written between 1739 and 1741, but Bowmer believes 1736 a possible date, and I am sure he is right. As to Y, these notes were obviously made when he was reading Beveridge. There is also considerable exact verbal agreement between Wesley's descriptions of the book, in Y, and in the Journal for the days when he was studying it. We have already seen that X provides historical justification for the Prudential Duties, the Stations and Lent, in MS. Y, and it deals with other matters which profoundly concerned him in September/October 1736. The historical information used in assessing the Canons, in MS. X was probably drawn from Beveridge, from Cave's *Primitive Christianity* which he had just read, and possibly from Cotelerius's *Apostolic Fathers*, which he read at the end of this period.

CHAPTER FOUR

Evangelical Conversion and Ecumenical Motive

I   WESLEY RETURNED FROM GEORGIA CONSCIOUS OF FAILURE

a *Failure in Holiness*

He had constructed a conception of holiness from 'Comprehensive' sources. He felt the Fathers of the first three centuries had guided him to what was central in Scriptural holiness, and he confirmed this from writings from the recent three centuries. Admittedly, he responded warmly to 'Catholic' writers—High Churchmen, and Romanic mystics, from Britain and the Continent—largely under the guidance of Non-Jurors. He had, however, been helped by British and Continental Protestants. Indeed, the sermons of a High Churchman, and an Arian whom he interpreted in loyal Trinitarian ways, assisted him to surround sister Hetty in her trouble with Christ's universal love. Nevertheless, in spite of such 'Comprehensive' inspirations, he felt that in Georgia he had failed to be holy in holy orders, and to achieve that unity in the Church for which he still yearned on the eve of his conversion.

b *Failure in Faith*

Jeremy Taylor's hesitancy, his mother's questioning of his hope of salvation, Deacon's dismissal of Purgatory and the consequent emphasis on holiness as essential in *this* life, and fear of storm and death on both Atlantic voyages, awakened him to his need of faith. Francke, the Lutheran Pietist, by his book *On the Fear of Man*, questioned his conversion and dared him to be a missionary. Finally, contact with the confident Moravians, and the account of the sudden conversion of Haliburton, the Scottish Presbyterian, caused him to arrive home seeking a faith which would bring peace through pardon, and power for holy living.

II   SAVING FAITH AND ECUMENICAL LOVE

With the help of Continental Protestants, Wesley found saving faith. Peter Bohler, a Pietist who had become a Moravian, convinced him that saving faith is not just faith in God, but faith in Christ, especially in Christ crucified, in Christ *alone*, renouncing dependence on one's own righteousness. The first-fruit of this faith is *peace through pardon*. A sinner can 'know' and 'feel' his sins forgiven. *Assurance* comes when the Spirit witnesses to pardon and acceptance. The second fruit is *power over sins*; the *power to pursue Christian perfection* by faith in Christ's power to perfect us in love. Wesley was convinced this experience was Scriptural, contemporary, and could be instantaneous, and so he sought it in all the means of grace.

The complete account of Wesley's conversion ought always to be read. Of 24 May 1738 he said, 'In the evening, I went very unwillingly to a society in Aldersgate Street, where one was reading Luther's *Preface to the Epistle to the Romans*. About a quarter before nine, while he was describing the change which God works in the heart through faith in Christ, I felt I did trust in Christ, Christ alone, for Salvation; and an assurance was given me that he had taken away *my* sins, even mine, and saved *me* from the law of sin and death'. Wesley found also ecumenical love. 'I began to pray with all my might for those who had in a more especial manner despitefully used me and persecuted me.' The Grand Jury of August 1737 had been loaded against him. Its forty-four members included 'a Papist . . . an infidel, three Baptists, 16 or 17 other Dissenters', and several others, doubtless Churchmen, all of whom had vowed vengeance. Rights and wrongs here are irrelevant. Pardoned himself, he received power to love those whose religious aims were antagonistic to his own.

À Kempis had led him to find in Matthew 5 the mind of the Master on holiness as inward: Jeremy Taylor helped him to hear the Lord in Matthew 6 demanding purity of intention: through William Law he heard Christ's command in the final verses of Matthew 5, 'Be ye therefore perfect, even as your Father which is in heaven': 'Love . . . and pray for them which despitefully use you and persecute you'. By faith in God's universal love in Christ, universal love really had come.

Universal love is the great ethical motive. It is the great evangelistic motive. Will the Lord kindle it again as a threefold flame when we really do express it, with Wesley, as ecumenical love?

CHAPTER FIVE

The Evangelical 'Catholic' Mission

1738–1750

SOME Evangelicals claim Wesley's conversion almost immediately cancelled his 'Catholic' convictions. Some 'Catholics' assert that his conversion was comparatively unimportant. Actually, this 'Catholic' of the first three centuries, now 'converted', aimed at leading a comprehensive mission to his homeland.

I THE DOUBLY APOSTOLIC SOURCES OF WESLEY'S AUTHORITY

In November 1738 Wesley opposed the introduction of lay moral supervisors, like the Moravian monitors, in the Fetter Lane Band-Society. This was for two reasons:

(i) '*The National Church* to which we belong may . . . claim some obedience from us.' On this ground he secured the observance of the Friday fast there, and later in his own Bristol and Foundery Societies, and he relaxed later even his own Non-Juror-inspired Wednesday fast. His Rules for the United Societies in 1743 just demand 'fasting', and he never ceased to appeal for some fasting, but he evidently regarded even Lent as Prudential, because not prescribed in the first three centuries.

(ii) 'I believe *bishops, priests and deacons* to be *of divine appointment* . . . *The Primitive Church*, may . . . be reverenced as faithfully delivering down for two or three hundred years, *the discipline* . . . *received from the Apostles*, and they from Christ.' The Wesleys continued to assert the Apostolic authority of their ministry by rebaptizing Dissenters by immersion on the basis of the book by Lawrence the Non-Juror on Lay Baptism, until possibly a good deal later than January 1739 when even Whitefield believed he 'would bring many (Dissenters) over to our communion' in this way. (Clarke, *Wesley Family*, ii, pp. 110–11.) However, rebaptism was a Prudential Practice, and by 1742, as we shall see, Wesley had secured what he regarded as the essential reality—an Apostolic Methodist discipline.

(iii) His *'extraordinary call'*. By this he justified his preaching in other men's parishes in a letter to Charles (23 June 1739), and it was the basis of his claim in March 1739 that 'I look upon all the world as my parish'. He and his helpers were 'extraordinary messengers' (Minutes 1744), and he thought of them as evangelists. Apostles, evangelists and prophets were the extraordinary Church officers, regarded as having ceased. We could call this, his 'Evangelical Apostolate'. (See E. W. Thompson's *'Wesley—Apostolic Man'*.) It did not displace, but fused with his 'Catholic' sense of authority, both together enabling him to travel beyond the limits authorized by ordinary Anglican authority.

II   GRACE, AND ADMISSION TO THE METHODIST SOCIETIES

God qualified a sinner for admission to the Methodist Society by granting prevenient grace, which prepared him for conversion. Wesley regarded the Foundery

Society, which began at the end of 1739, as the first true Methodist Society. Its qualification for admission became that for Methodism: 'A desire to flee from the wrath to come, to be saved from their sin'. Rebaptism of Dissenters was not even suggested.

God also gave Justifying Faith which qualified 'Believers' for admission to the *Bands*. Finally, some were admitted to the *Select Society*, having received *Sanctifying Grace*, power to pursue or possess Christian Perfection, so that they were patterns of love and holiness. May God renew his gifts of repentance, of peace through pardon, and of power to pursue perfection in this needy twentieth century.

III   The Means of Grace, and Continuance in the Societies

a *Attendance at the Ordained Means of Grace*

Scripture, read or expounded, prayer, private or public, and the Supper of the Lord, was required as evidence of the *continuing* desire of members of the Society for salvation. This was an outcome of the controversy of 1739–40 with Molther, the Pietistic Moravian who depreciated the means of grace, and claimed that only fully converted people should communicate. Wesley, in asserting that 'preventing, justifying, or sanctifying grace' could come in the means, was in line with Article XXV, but in declaring that all repentant sinners could come he made admission to the Society, and therefore to the sacrament, not only wider than the Independents, and Anglicans, but even than the Primitive Church! He called ordinary Society members 'catechumens'—and catechumens were not admitted to communion in the Primitive Church. They were not justified believers. Dissenters and former 'heathen' now entered the Society, as well as Churchmen, making some kind of wider Comprehension ultimately necessary.

b *Prudential Means*

In these earlier years, Wesley gathered many valuable Prudential Practices from various sections of the Christian Church, thus making the total religious provision for Anglican and Dissenting Methodists more comprehensive. The Moravians at this time were his major source of fresh values, contributing to Methodism their Bands, Love-feasts, and Watch-nights. They shared with Whitefield and Howell Harris in inspiring Wesley's Field-preaching, with Harris and Susanna Wesley and others in justifying lay preaching, and with Dissenters in adding extempore prayer to Wesley's Anglican forms. Wesley shaped new practices for himself, and reshaped these older practices in new ways. Non-Juror inspired exorcisms tended to decrease, but Wesley saw parallels to some of his innovations, in the Primitive Church. His 5 a.m. services were 'cock-crow' services: sick-visitors were 'Deaconesses': Class-members were 'Catechumens' and Band-members were the 'Faithful': the Love-feast was the 'Agape': and the Watch-nights were the 'Vigils', of the Primitive Church. In Georgia, Wesley produced his hymns under direct Moravian inspiration, but borrowed others from many sources. With these examples in his mind and the joy of his conversion in his heart, Charles Wesley commenced to overflow with the hymns of the Revival. All these were additional means of conveying 'preventing, justifying and sanctifying grace'.[1]

[1] In 1937 I wrote the Eayrs' Prize Essay on 'The Influence of Moravianism on Methodism'. That great Methodist layman, Dr C. W. Towlson, made use of this in his *Moravian and Methodist*. Readers of that book must remember that lay preaching led to our brotherhood of ministerial as well as local preachers.

IV   THE APOSTOLIC DISCIPLINE—ADMISSIONS AND EXCLUSIONS

a *Society Members*

In February 1741 Wesley tried one method of discipline, consulting bands at Bristol as to the retention of Society members. The description is closely parallel to the similar procedure in the Apostolical Constitutions. (II 37; 41; 47; 58.) He issued class tickets. These were required for admission to Love-feasts and the Lord's Table. This 'fencing of the Table' and the method were similar to the practice of the Primitive Church.

In February 1741 he also excluded some from Kingswood 'by the consent and approbation of the band-society', which sounds like an old Presbyterian formula. Consequently when the Society was first divided under class leaders, Wesley said, 'This is the thing, the very thing we have wanted so long'. From then on he consulted class leaders about issuing or withholding tickets, the final decision being his own, in harmony with the authority of the Bishop in the Apostolical Constitutions. (II 11; 37; 47.) He then believed the Primitive Bishop (unlike a Presbyterian like Baxter) had a wider than local authority, similar to his own ever-widening responsibility for discipline.

b *The Bands—a New Testament Confessional*

Wesley substituted bands for the Non-Juror-inspired Georgian confession, changing the spontaneous Moravian practice into a voluntarily accepted rule. Members made personal confession in the small group of married, or single, men, or women. (Wesley did not rule out voluntary confession 'to a priest'.) They prayed for one another. There was 'exhortation' particularly from the lay leader. The purpose was spiritual therapy—'that we may be healed'.

c *Penitents—without Penances*

When band members fell into sin, Wesley met them as Penitents. He imposed no such penances as Deacon urged in his 'Penitential Office', which he may have used in Georgia, but he did follow the Ancient Church in appointing a special service for them, with appropriate hymns, exhortations and prayers. One could draw out at length the way his description applies to Deacon's 'Office'. Wesley also says he 'endeavoured to bring them back to the great Shepherd and *Bishop* of their souls'. Is this a consciously higher aim than that of the '*Bishop*' who was 'to restore (the Penitent) . . . to his ancient place among the flock'? (Apostolical Constitutions II 41.) Again, the power to restore the penitent to the Band was Wesley's own.

d *The Select Society*

The Select Society with members so possessed by perfect love as to be patterns of holiness, reminded the whole Society that—like men in holy orders, and like the Catholic Church—Methodism existed to produce holiness.

Wesley held that his power of admitting to and excluding from Societies and Bands was his basic power. It was Apostolic and Episcopal in the sense that it was wider than local. Later he shared this episcopé with his assistants, and the 1784 Deed of Declaration passed the final power to Conference. Discipline in Methodism today is more balanced and democratic, but this tougher and Apostolic Discipline checked smuggling in Cornwall, thieving from wrecked vessels in Ireland, and spurred members on through forgiveness towards the holiness of perfect universal love. Behind it originally was the personal leadership of Wesley reinforced by the authority he believed he had received by Apostolic Succession from the Apostles, and also by the 'extraordinary call' of this 'Apostolic man'. In June 1739 Wesley secured legal control of the Bristol New Room, a procedure which led to the later Model Deeds. In 1744 he commenced his annual Conferences under partial Moravian inspiration. The legal and administrative connexional direction inherited by Conference from Wesley, which has given unity to Methodism, has behind it this personal, and doubly 'Apostolic' conviction of Wesley.

V   The Evangelical 'Catholic' Mission

a *A High Church Appeal for Unity in Mission*

In 1742 Wesley published *The Character of a Methodist*, and Charles's great hymn 'Wrestling Jacob'. Later, in Wesley's great hymnbook, one line was printed in capitals, that great climactic line of this hymn—'PURE, UNIVERSAL LOVE THOU ART'. In his manifesto, this great ecumenical and evangelistic motive inspired Wesley to plead with all orthodox Protestants, with whom he identified the Methodists, for sympathy and even support on his widening mission. The aims of the Methodist, holiness of heart and life, springing from true faith, are 'the common, fundamental principles of Christianity'. 'Let real Christians of whatsoever denomination . . . be in no way divided. Opinions which distinguish real, orthodox Christians must not 'destroy the work of God . . . Let us strive together for the faith of the Gospel'. This was the appeal to London, the west and the north, of a High Churchman, who firmly believed in Apostolic Succession, Justification by Faith and the believing pursuit of holiness in this life. Would to God Apostolic ministers of either kind, could lead the Church in commending Christ's central contribution to this country in this twentieth century!

b *A 'Catholic' Evangelical Alternative Communion*

In 1745 the Wesleys published *Hymns on the Lord's*

63

Supper.[1] We are content to stress that here Evangelical, and 'Catholic' in the Non-Juror sense, are perfectly fused in a Communion intended to convert sinners to saints. We ignore Brevint's fine outline and simply show how these hymns could be used for an alternative Communion from the Consecration Prayer onwards.

(i) Hymn 1 could be used in place of the account of *the Institution* of the Lord's Supper contained in the Consecration Prayer. It uses 'blessed' as in the 1549 Prayer Book favoured by the Non-Jurors, thus preparing for the Invocation—'He took, and *bless'd*, and brake the bread'.

(ii) *The Anamnesis.* This is the act by which, in the section on this 'Memorial of the Sufferings and Death of Christ' we *'recall to mind'* (20 v. 1), not only Christ's Passion and Death, but also One who has mounted to 'glory . . . in Sion's height', (19 and 20) and will 'to judgement come'. (12 vv. 1 and 3.) Deacon, the Apostolical Constitutions and the Orthodox Church, remember Christ's Passion and Death, but also his Resurrection, Ascension and Second Coming in Judgement.

Dr Gordon Rupp emphasizes that Charles Wesley believed this saving 'Remembrance of Calvary is only possible in the Holy Spirit', and effectively quoted Hymn 16 (MHB 765) 'Come, Thou everlasting Spirit'. The Epiclesis in the Apostolical Constitutions, prays for the Spirit as *'the witness of our Lord Jesus's sufferings'*, echoed by Deacon, and by the next verse in the hymn:

> Come, *Thou witness of His dying*,
> Come, Remembrancer Divine,
> Let us feel Thy power, applying
> Christ to every soul, and mine.

[1] See the books already mentioned, by Bowmer and Parris, and also the book about these hymns by Dr Rattenbury, who was aware of some of their Non-Juror elements, but not of their Non-Juror origin. Some of the elements mentioned above have not previously been detected.

64

(iii) *The Anamnesis includes the 'Offering'.* (124 v. 2.)
Wesley alters Brevint's title of this section, 'Concerning the Sacrament, as it is a Sacrifice', to 'The Holy *Eucharist* as it implies a Sacrifice'. Deacon calls his Liturgy '. . . The Form of *Offering* the Sacrifice . . . of the *Eucharist*', and the last name is not in the Prayer Books we have covered. In these hymns, the sacrifice of Christ alone atones. The 'offering' on this 'Altar' is not made by a priest acting alone for others, but by the whole Church acting in these priestly hymns. Wesley uses 'celebrate', a verb not found in Brevint, but in the oblatory sentence in the 1549 Prayer Book:

> Yet may we *celebrate* below,
> And daily thus Thine *offering* show. (124 v. 2.)

Just as Non-Jurors gave a sacrificial interpretation to 'do' in our Lord's command, which Deacon renders, '*Do* this for a memorial of me', so Charles sings,

> We . . . *Do* as Jesus bids us *do*
> Signify His flesh and blood,
> Him in a *memorial* show,
> *Offer* up the Lamb to God.
>> (118 v. 4. See also MHB 723.)

(iv) *The Invocation* was provided in 72 (MHB 767).

> Come, Holy Ghost, Thine influence shed,
> And realize the sign;
> Thy *life* infuse into the bread,
> Thy *power* into the wine.
>
> *Effectual* let the tokens prove,
> And *made*, by heavenly art,
> Fit channels to convey Thy love,
> To every faithful heart.

The hymns are based on *The Christian Sacrament and Sacrifice* by Dr Brevint (1616–95).

Parris shows that Wesley travels beyond Brevint, and that for 'life' and 'power' Wesley turned to J. Johnson's *The Unbloody Sacrifice*, the source of the Non-Jurors' Eucharistic theology. Parris calls Wesley's doctrine virtualism. This denies 'any change in the elements took place, but . . . the faithful receive the power or virtue of the body and blood of Christ'. Grisbrooke calls the Non-Jurors' doctrine 'dynamic virtualism'. Let us turn to experience. On the decisive day when Charles Wesley commenced field-preaching (24 June 1739) he said that at St Paul's, 'Psalms, Lessons, &c. . . . and the sacrament . . . put fresh *life* into me'. Let theologians define and controversialists contrast—and all Christians use all the means of grace.

(v) *Hymns about the Mixture* of Water and Wine (74 and 75) illustrate the fusion of the Evangelical and Catholic found everywhere in these hymns. Justifying and sanctifying grace can come with bread or cup:

> The sin-atoning blood apply,
> And let the water sanctify,
> Pardon and holiness impart. (31 v. 2.)

(vi) In 20 (MHB 181), after addressing the 'Lamb of God' as in *the Gloria in excelsis* (which is in the early position of 20 in the 1549 Prayer Book, and the Roman Mass, but was moved to the end of the Communion in 1552, where it remained in the 1662 Book), Charles thought of *the Dismissal sentence* which Non-Jurors drew from the New Testament through the Apostolical Constitutions, and so ends each verse: 'O remember Calvary, and bid us *go in peace*.' Dismissal Sentences have never been printed in Methodist Orders of Communion. Of fifty-seven ministers of all former sections of Methodism, fifty told me they prefix 'Go in peace . . . ' and forty add something like 'and the God of peace go with thee'. The

Rev. E. P. F. Scholes said he thought this was the invariable Methodist practice in 1895! This ancient tradition probably derived from Wesley.

This Catholic—Evangelical Alternative Communion, published nine times by Wesley, is not official Methodist doctrine, but admits us to the devotional life of the two Evangelists, who at the Table of the Lord saw sinners receive peace through pardon, and power to pursue perfection.

c *A Moderate Episcopalian's Appeal for Unity in Mission*

On 30 December 1745 Wesley wrote a letter to his brother-in-law Westley Hall, declaring his belief in the outward priesthood and sacrifice, Anglican sacraments being valid because of a commission from bishops in succession from the Apostles. We do well to remember that this High Churchman had preached already the chief Standard Sermons which set forth his evangelical doctrines.

On 20 January 1746 he read King's *Account of the Primitive Church* (1691), which says the New Testament bishop was head of a parish, not a diocese, and that presbyters were different in degree from the bishops, but not in order, each being subject to his bishop but having the same powers. Wesley did not accept this at the time, for the 1747 Conference Minutes declare the threefold Order is 'plainly described in the New Testament' and 'generally obtained in . . . the Apostolic age', although not designed by God to obtain through all ages, for 'it is (not) asserted in Holy Writ', and the foreign reformed Churches must be parts of the Church of Christ. He was still wrestling with King, but had become a moderate Episcopalian.

In 1939 I advanced the theory that in 1749 Wesley derived the Circuit Quarterly Meeting, which has helped to promote unity of smaller families of churches, from the Quaker Quarterly Meeting, through John Bennet. Dr Frank Baker has now given exciting confirmation of this. At the same time, I claimed the Quakers also inspired Wesley with the idea of a 'general union of our Societies throughout England', the London Society to be considered the Mother Church, a telescoping of the concept of the Quaker Yearly or London Meeting, with their Meeting of Sufferings. It was a pity it was not pursued, but it is another illustration of Wesley's search for unity, and for values from other denominations. Similarly he triumphed over the Arminian/Calvinistic division by effecting an agreement with Whitefield and Howell Harris in August 1749 for a 'Union in carrying on the Work of God'. On 8 September he followed up this limited achievement of unity by preaching on the text of his great 'Catholic Spirit' Sermon.

As in 'The Character of a Methodist', Wesley appeals to all Protestants save Anti-Trinitarians. He will not dispute about modes of worship or forms of Church government. Instead of such opinions, he sets before all Christians the supreme values of faith and love which ought to draw them together. Faith is more than orthodox Trinitarianism. Christ must 'dwell in thy heart by faith', which must work by whole-hearted love of God and all mankind. 'This is Catholic, or universal love . . . Run the race . . . in true Catholic love, till thou art swallowed up in love for ever and ever'. We must love fellow Christians. 'Join with me in the work of God.'

Wesley published this sermon in 1750, in the third volume of his Standard Sermons. Had he abandoned the ideal of unity which had fascinated him about twenty years before? He says he still believed his mode of worship (which meant the Book of Common Prayer, supplemented by extempore prayer and the Sacramental Hymns), to be 'truly primitive and apostolical', and 'the Episcopal form of Church-government to be scriptural and apostolical'. But he dared not 'impose' his opinions and practices on others. 'We will talk of these things, if need be, at a more convenient season.' If 'an entire external union' could not then be secured, let all co-operate in faith and love, in mission to the homeland. Despair about unity could have been justified. The Church of England Convocations were silenced from 1717 until 1854. How could a Church with no co-ordinating Council effectively co-ordinate orthodox Protestantism? In his Sermon of 1786 on 'Schism' Wesley said, 'Happy is . . . the peacemaker in the Church of God . . . Labour after this . . . The God of peace is on your side . . . Never be weary . . . in due time thou shalt reap, if thou faint not.'

CHAPTER SIX

The Comprehension of Values of Independency, Presbyterianism, and Episcopacy

1750–1764

In this period, Wesley turned afresh to the proposals made for the Comprehension of Dissent and the Church of England at the Restoration and Revolution, and also studied the New Testament doctrine of the Ministry, each shedding light on the other.

I INDEPENDENCY AND PRESBYTERIANISM

In 1751–2 seven of Wesley's preachers became Independent ministers. This is the true contemporary background to that part of his Journal published in 1753 in which he says of King's book on the Primitive Church, read in 1746, that if this book were true, 'bishops and presbyters are (essentially) of one order, and that originally every Christian congregation was a church independent of all others'. Independency as an implication of the parity of the ministry was unwelcome to Wesley. The solution of the practical problem it posed was reached at the Conference in May 1754, when the preachers 'all willingly signed an agreement (or Covenant?) not to act independently of each other'.

Typical of this period was the Covenant Service,[1] first effectively introduced to his Societies by Wesley in August 1755. The actual covenant was composed by Joseph Alleine, a young Presbyterian minister, for use in 1658 by a group of young converts. Joseph's father-in-law included it in his *Vindiciae Pietatis, or Vindication of Godliness* written in 1663. Anticipating repression after the Act of Uniformity, he urged older Christians to use this young convert's covenant. Presbyterians had made national covenants. Independents organized their 'gathered churches' by making church covenants. Independency at its best can show the Christian world the wonder of a local Church directly governed by the will of Christ. At that time, Independents and Presbyterians were drawn closer together. In 1663, Joseph became friendly with an ardent Independent, John Westley, grandfather of John and Charles. (Wesley said covenanting was practised by 'our forefathers'.) Perhaps Richard's idea of using this covenant, for 'the saints', sprang from this friendship of Presbyterian and Independent. Certainly the Wesleys called the Methodists to make their personal covenant as part of the corporate commitment of the whole Society. In Charles's hymns, 'we offer' at Communion, and in the Covenant Service we

> . . . all, with one accord,
> In a perpetual covenant join
> Ourselves to Christ the Lord.

> (MHB 749.)

The modern revised form of the Covenant Service is a Methodist contribution to the Prayer Book of the Church of South India. It is fascinating that the Congregationalists who have stressed local autonomy, and Presbyterians

[1] See my article in the *London Quarterly*, January 1939.

who accept the direction of Christ through wider representative bodies, are today being drawn together through the concept of covenanting, common to both communions.

II   INDEPENDENCY, PRESBYTERIANISM, AND EPISCOPACY

a *Presbyterian Influences*

In April 1754, Wesley read Calamy's 'Abridgement of Mr Baxter's Life'. Later, I shall argue that partly under the inspiration of this book Wesley took account of the suggested revisions of the Presbyterians in 1661, when revising the Book of Commmon Prayer, in his 'Sunday Service' of 1784. In August 1754, he also read Baxter's *History of the Councils*. In 1754–5 he expressed sympathy, in letters, with the objections of the Presbyterians of 1661, as recorded by Calamy, to the Liturgy, Canons and Spiritual Courts of the Established Church. In January 1754 Wesley commenced his *Notes on the New Testament*, completing them shortly after September 1755. These Notes yearn for unity. Matthew 5:47 is in the paragraph which includes 'pray for them that despitefully use you' which inspired his conversion-day prayer for forgiveness for his 'Christian' enemies of various denominations. On these verses he laments 'the unhappy divisions and subdivisions into which Christ's church has been crumbled'. He prays 'that we might cordially embrace our brethren in Christ, of whatever party or denomination'. The scholars he studied for his comments included a Presbyterian Lutheran, a High Churchman and two Independents, but King, Baxter, Calamy, and Stillingfleet, all interested in Comprehension, also influenced him. He knew the divisive power of emotive terms. In his Preface, (dated 4 January 1754) he cries, 'Would to God that all the party names and unscriptural phrases and forms, which have divided the Christian world were forgot; and that we might all agree to sit down together, as humble loving disciples, at the feet of our common Master'. These Notes are Methodist Standards.

b *Wesley's Conception of the Christian Ministry*

(i) On Philippians 1:1 he says, 'The word bishops here includes all the presbyters at Philippi, as well as the ruling presbyters: the names bishop and presbyter, or elder, being *promiscuously* used in the first ages'. On this same text, Stillingfleet shows that 'bishop' and 'presbyter' are synonymous, and that the name 'presbyter' is taken *promiscuously* both for 'bishop' and 'presbyter'.[1] Stillingfleet wrote his *Irenicon* in 1659, advocating Anglican recognition of Presbyterian ministries and acceptance by Presbyterians of a moderate Episcopacy. The above quotations show that *this moderate Bishop* confirmed Wesley's acceptance of King's view that in the New Testament, 'presbyters and bishops are (essentially) of one order'.

E. W. Thompson says that Wesley made no reference to King's idea that there are different grades in New Testament bishops. (*Wesley—Apostolic Man* pp. 28–30.) It has also been said that Wesley's comment on Acts 20:17, 'Perhaps elders and bishops were then the same, or no otherwise different than are the rector of a parish and his curates', wavers between two theories, but actually, he draws this parallel almost verbally from King! (King pp. 53–4.) Thus from the *Presbyterian* he draws acknowledgment of the difference, at least in grade, between New Testament presbyters!

[1] See A. B. Lawson's *John Wesley and the Christian Ministry*, pp. 66–7, the fullest and latest book on this subject, indispensable for those studying this subject. Compare my evidence, and assessment of it, critically with his, and my very different conclusions. I underline my tribute.

(ii) In Romans 12:8 Wesley translates the Greek word for 'he that ruleth' as 'he that presideth', adding 'That hath the care of the flock'. In 1773 he used this Greek word in urging Fletcher to be his personal successor, 'to *preside* over all Methodists'. In the 'presiding elder' perhaps he already saw an anticipation of later, wider Presidencies.

(iii) He believed the Apostle had the wider New Testament episcopé. On Acts 1:20, 'Let his bishopric another take' (A.V.) he says, 'That is, his apostleship'. He implies that an apostle was like a diocesan bishop, for on Paul's claim in Acts 20:34, 'These hands have ministered to my necessities, and to them that were with me', he asks, 'Who . . . envies such a bishop, or archbishop as this?'. He says 'archbishop' because in the next verse he refers to the New Testament bishops, or episcopoi. On Paul's excommunication of the gravely immoral member in 1 Corinthians 5: 3–4, he says, 'the passing of this sentence was the act of the apostle, not of the Corinthians'. In effect he justified the diocesan bishop and the presbyters in sharing in ordination, by an apparent correction of King's exposition of 1 Timothy 4:14, 'Neglect not the gift that is in thee, which was given thee by prophecy, with the laying on of the hands of the presbytery'. He points out from 2 Timothy 1:6 that Paul, (the Apostle who had wider powers), shared in this ordination. The Superintendent in Wesley's 1784 'Sunday Service', like the Anglican Bishop, followed this precedent. Wesley therefore combined the theory of King and Stillingfleet, that in the New Testament presbyter and episcopos are synonymous, with Stillingfleet's belief that the wider and greater powers of the diocesan bishop were not new since the apostles had these powers.

This explains why, in 1755, Wesley re-issued his *Book of Prayers* of 1733, presumably as a re-affirmation of his belief in the value of 'Bishops, Priests and Deacons',

74

but on a different theory. In 1756 he wrote, 'I still believe the Episcopal form of Church government to be both Scriptural and apostolical: I mean, well agreeing with the practice and writings of the Apostles. But that it is pre-scribed in Scripture I do not believe. This opinion (which I once heartily espoused) I have been heartily ashamed of ever since I read Dr Stillingfleet's *Irenicon*. I think he has unanswerably proved that Christ nor His Apostles prescribed any particular form of Church government.' (Letters III, p. 182.) In a letter probably of this time he wrote, 'I do not see that Diocesan Episcopacy is necessary but I do that it is highly expedient . . . The Apostles had not the Lordships . . . but they had the office of Diocesan Bishops.' (Lawson, ibid p. 78.)

(iv) Almost certainly at this time he rejected 'uninter-rupted Apostolic Succession'—even although he did not publicly renounce it until February 1761—in controversy with a Roman Catholic priest, when he wrote that he 'could never see it proved . . . (that) the Romish bishops came down by uninterrupted succession from the Apostles . . . and I am persuaded I never shall'. (Letters 4, pp. 135ff. See his *Notes on the New Testament* on Romans 16:5.) Stillingfleet says slyly of Rome, 'Here the succes-sion is as muddy as the Tiber itself'. (Ibid p. 322.)

(v) There is a gap in Wesley's explanation. He nowhere says when or how the Apostles' wider-than-local author-ity was recommenced in the diocesan episcopate. Is there a presumption that here, too, he would follow Stillingfleet?

However, we see that his theory is a partial comprehen-sion of Independent, Presbyterian, and Episcopal views.

III   MAINTENANCE AND DEVELOPMENT OF UNITY

a *Maintenance of Unity with the Church of England*
There was a tension between Wesley's extraordinary

call to proclaim the Gospel, and his desire for unity. It is therefore right to describe the debate of these years as being concerned with 'Separation from the Church'. The pressure to ordain was real. He wondered whether it was lawful for 'presbyters circumstanced as we are, to ordain'. He eventually decided that ordination was not expedient. He published his *Preservative Against Unsettled Notions in Religion* in 1758 to defend his young preachers against Deists, Socinians, Arians, Papists, and Mystics, also to show where he stood in respect to Quakers, Baptists, and Moravians. He re-asserted that the supreme values are 'love of God and man, and holiness of heart and life'.

The firm decision of 1758 not to separate from the Church of England, meant that Methodist meetings were not to compete with Church of England worship and communion, which 'Church Methodists' were expected to attend. In a letter of January 1758, he argued with Towgood, a moderate Arian Presbyterian minister, that Christ has not forbidden the Church 'a power of decreeing rites and ceremonies . . . purely indifferent', and, therefore, 'we need not separate from the Church in order to preserve our allegiance to Christ, but may be firm members thereof'. In his *Reasons against Separation from the Church of England* of 1758, he said Methodists were not 'a particular sect'. They were 'debtors to all who are Christians in name but heathens in heart . . . of whatever denomination . . . for their good'. He firmly decided against dissenting, and yet identified himself with, and appealed to both Dissenters and Anglicans.

b *Appeals for Evangelical Unity*

Feeling now that the narrower appeal might yield greater results, he campaigned for unity in mission of the more Evangelical Christians. The 1757 Conference discussed the possibility of 'a close union with the clergy, who preach the truth'. His *Treatise on Original Sin* (1757) used the writings of a Scottish Presbyterian, two Independents, and an Anglican Calvinist, and in 1761, he added Original Sin to Justification and Love, as the basis of co-operation for the Evangelicals. (Letters 4 p. 235). In 1764 he circularized fifty or sixty Evangelical clergy, asking that 'each help the other on in his work'. Twelve attended the 1764 Conference, and, with Charles Wesley, wanted the preachers withdrawn from parishes where the incumbent preached the Gospel. Wesley refused, as the Methodists would not have 'all the advantages for holiness' they enjoyed, and the incumbent might not be able to discipline them. (Myles, *Chronological History*, p. 95.) He began to think more about Methodist unity. Did he abandon the wider ideal?

CHAPTER SEVEN

Accepting Episcopacy or
Assuming Episcopal Powers

1763–1775

I   ACCEPTING EPISCOPACY

a *The Lord's Supper from an Orthodox Methodist Priest!*

Maxfield, ordained by an Irish bishop to assist Wesley by administering communion in London, left Wesley in April 1763 for the Church of England. In the same year, Wesley asked John Jones, a scholarly Methodist lay-preacher, to write to the Greek Orthodox Patriarch at Smyrna, who confirmed the genuineness of a certain Bishop Erasmus, saying he was Bishop of Arcadia in Crete. At Wesley's request, Erasmus ordained Jones priest. The Very Reverend George Tsoumas, a priest of the Greek Orthodox Church, states that Erasmus was not a canonical bishop of that Church, but honours Wesley's honest belief that he was. Wesley's honesty means his action is reliable evidence of his attitude towards Episcopacy and the Orthodox Church.

Charles Wesley would not let Jones assist him in administering the sacrament, and he had to stop. Tyerman suggests that almost immediately Jones entered the Church of England, but in fact he did not leave Methodism until 1767. A letter of 1 March 1764 from John to Charles, shows that with the advice of the London stewards, John was determined to have Jones's assistance during his absence in Scotland, and T. Olivers, in his defence of Wesley's actions, written in 1771, says Jones did administer the Lord's Supper (see p. 80). Did Wesley have the brief satisfaction of feeling that through the Non-Juror Usages in the Sacramental Hymns, Dr Jones drew London Methodists nearer to the Primitive, and to the Greek Orthodox, Churches?

b *An Orthodox Methodist Succession?*

Tyerman claims that Mather was ordained by Erasmus. He was ordained Superintendent by Wesley in 1788. Had he commenced a succession some might have been pleased by this partial and uncertain connexion with Greek Orthodoxy. However, Tyerman was certainly wrong, but, on the same shaky foundation, we might have had:

c *An Orthodox Methodist Worker-Priest?*

Tyerman misunderstood a Press report of the ordination of 'a master baker' as referring to Mather, when Staniforth was certainly meant. Other Methodist preachers had secured ordination from the obliging Erasmus. Because money may have been paid, and they did not understand the language in which he ordained, and because they acted without Wesley's own authority, Wesley disowned them all early in 1765. The Greek Orthodox Church ordain some priests who also continue their daily employment. Although Staniforth was naïve in this matter, and although he never acted on his ordination, as he was a *local* preacher, and therefore potentially the first Methodist 'worker-priest'—or 'presbyter'?—we commend him to Luton Industrial College!

d *Wesley Recognized the Value of a Wider Acceptance of Episcopally-ordained Ministries*

In 1771, Toplady attacked Wesley about the Greek

ordinations, saying that Jones ' "could only be a Minister of the Greek Church, which could give him no legal right to act as a Minister of the Church of England". Thomas Olivers answered Mr Toplady in a publication *by the consent of Mr Wesley*. He said, "1. The Doctor did not *officiate as* a clergyman of the Church of England, but as an assistant to Mr Wesley, in preaching, and administering the Lord's Supper in his Societies. 2. Whoever is episcopally ordained, is a Minister of the Church universal, and as such has a right to officiate in any part of the globe. 3. This all Episcopalians who understand their doctrines know; hence it is that the Church of *England* frequently employs, without re-ordination, priests ordained even by *Popish* Bishops. 4. Any Bishop in England will acknowledge the validity of the ordination of a Popish Priest by a Popish Bishop." ' (Myles, *Chronological History*, p. 76.) This very important statement is omitted by Tyerman and all who depend on him. One certificate issued by Erasmus to 'a priest', spoke of his 'power to minister . . . in all the world'. Wesley himself claimed the right to act universally on the same basis, and asserts the same right here through Olivers.

The Wesleys had helped to secure Anglican recognition for Moravian orders. Wesley's claim that Orthodox ordinations were on a par with Roman ordinations was a challenge to the English bishops, for, although Archbishop Wake had repudiated the approaches of the Non-Jurors to the Russian Orthodox Church in 1725, he had done nothing effective about the relations of the two Churches, and it was not until 1908 that provision was made for members of the Greek Orthodox Church to receive Anglican communion if they could not receive it from their own priests. Wesley was not saying that the validity of sacraments depended on episcopal ordination. He was recognizing the practical situation, even although he admitted Dissenters himself, that episcopal ordination already and potentially afforded wider opportunities for communion. It is not impossible that he had not forgotten this in 1784.

e *Why not an Orthodox- or Anglican-Methodist Bishop?*

Toplady asked Wesley, '3. Did you not strongly press this supposed Greek Bishop to consecrate you a bishop, that you might be invested with a power of ordaining what ministers you pleased, to officiate in your societies as clergymen? And did he not refuse to consecrate you, alleging this for his reason,—That, according to the canons of the Greek church, more than one bishop must be present to assist at the consecration of a new one?'

Olivers' reply to 3 (given with Wesley's consent) was, 'No. But suppose he had? Where would have been the blame? Mr Wesley is connected with a number of persons who have given every proof, which the nature of the thing allows, that they have an *inward call* to preach the gospel. Both he, and they would be glad if they had an *outward call* too. But no bishop in *England* will give it them. What wonder then, if he was to endeavour to procure it by any other innocent means?' (*Olivers' Letters to Toplady*, 1771, p. 50.)

Wesley probably confirmed from Erasmus that three Orthodox bishops consecrated another, having in mind that only one Moravian bishop consecrated Seifart in Georgia, and that Paul was the only apostle who shared with the presbyters in ordaining Timothy, precedents he followed in his Ordinal of 1784 in arranging that one Superintendent with Elders could 'ordain' another Superintendent. Is not the implication of this defence that if consecration had been offered to Wesley by the Orthodox Church, or by the Church of England, he would have seriously considered it so that some of his men might have been ordained? It sounds like a direct public hint to the Bench of Bishops! Was he prepared to consider 'taking Episcopacy into the Methodist system'?

II 'WESLEY'S DESIGNATED SUCCESSOR'

We have told of Wesley's willingness in 1771 to consider consecration as a sequel to the Orthodox ordinations of 1763–4, but we must now consider it as a stage in Wesley's attempts to settle the future of Methodism after his death.

In 1768 Wesley issued Part 13 of his Journal which concludes with the account, by his grandfather, John Westley, of his examination by Bishop Ironside of Bristol, about his credentials, shortly before his ejection in 1662 from his work in Winterbourne Whitchurch, because he was not episcopally ordained.

First, this was a justification of lay-preaching. His grandfather was never ordained, but says he was approved by judicious Christians and ministers, and by God granting conversions to godliness, and that 'There has been more written in proof of preaching of gifted persons, with such approbation, than has been answered yet'. (Journal V, pp. 120–4.)

Second, Westley said he 'was called to the *work* of the ministry, though not the *office*'. He had been 'sent to preach the gospel' by the church at Melcombe, (which was Independent). This was the sending mentioned in Romans 10, of those 'who preach the gospel' or evangel, (v. 15), which the founder of Methodism interpreted as referred to 'evangelists'. As such Westley could preach, but he says that he was not called to 'the office' of the ministry, because the people of his church were 'not a people who are fit subjects for me to exercise office-work among them'. Only when a sufficient number of converts formed a gathered church by accepting a Church covenant, could an Independent Church begin its full sacramental life. John Wesley actually omits his grandfather's reference to the Independents, for he did not believe in full local autonomy, but he used this distinction in his Korah Sermon of 1789, claiming that evangelists had the right to preach but nowhere in the first three centuries had they the right of a pastor to administer the sacraments, and that his preachers as evangelists ought not to seek to be priests.

At the Conference in the following year, 1769, Wesley acknowledged he had failed to unite the Evangelical clergy, and asked how his preachers could maintain union after his death. He suggested they should then sign an agreement in London to act together, and choose a committee of three, five, or seven, each to be a Moderator in his turn. 'Let the Committee do what I do now; propose preachers to be tried, admitted or excluded; fix the place of each preacher for the ensuing year.' French Protestants derived the title 'Moderator' from the Gallican Church, and passed it on to Dutch and Scottish Protestants. It was used at Oxford and Cambridge Universities, and Ussher in his *Reduction of Episcopacy unto the Form of Synodical Government received in the Ancient Church* of 1641, suggested that Bishops and Primates should be Moderators of the Diocesan and Provincial Synods respectively. The title therefore was ecumenically inspired. Wesley suggested no arrangements for ordination. Why did he prefer the title 'Superintendent' in 1784?

It was two years after this that in 1771 Wesley seems to have thought that he ought perhaps to be offered an Anglican episcopé over Methodism. In December 1772 he appealed to Charles to help him at Conference: 'You could say something about the Church . . . If we live till August, stand by me, and we will put the matter home . . .

Let me be again an Oxford Methodist! I am often in doubt whether it would not be best to resume all my Oxford rules.' In logical development, Wesley wrote Fletcher in 1773, urging him to leave his parish in order to prepare to be his personal successor over Methodism in Britain and America. He quoted Homer: 'The rule of many is not good; let there be one ruler'. 'I see more and more, unless there be one πρωεστώς, the work can never be carried on. The body of preachers are not united; nor will any part of them submit to the rest: so that either there must be *one* to preside over *all*, or the work will indeed come to an end.' We met the cognate Greek word in Wesley's *Notes on the New Testament*, on 'he that presideth' in Romans 12:8 (see page 73). Later, in 1784, he arranged for Methodist Presidents.

This decade from 1763 onwards shows a consistent development of Wesley's thought in favour of a single leader of the Trans-Atlantic Methodist Society. In 1771 he seems to have thought such a leader would do even better work if granted Episcopal powers of ordination.

Fletcher refused to be his successor. From 1773 to 1775 a pledge of united action was signed in the successive Conferences, 101 preachers signing in all. What other plan for future Methodist unity could emerge?

III   METHODIST PRESBYTERAL APPOINTMENT, OR ORDINATION?

a *Benson's Plan*, 1775

Benson, a young preacher, obviously troubled, when in Edinburgh from 1773–4, by Presbyterian criticism of unordained preachers, wrote Fletcher in 1775, saying it would be good, '2. To set apart those who are judged qualified for the *work* of the ministry by fasting, prayer, and imposition of the hands of "the Wesleys" and other presbyters of the Established Church'. Apart from two important differences, this follows the current Scottish Presbyterian definition of ordination, as 'the solemn setting apart of a person to some publick church *office*. Every minister of the word is to be *ordained* by the imposition of hands, and prayer, with fasting, by those preaching presbyters to whom it doth belong.' Benson's son said Fletcher mistakenly thought Joseph Benson was proposing ordination. Is the explanation that he was following John Westley, Senior, and asked, not for *ordination* to the *office* with authority to administer sacraments, but to be *set apart* for the *work* of preaching? (After Wesley's death, Benson gave unity to the preachers by persuading them to accept appointment as the equivalent of ordination.) If so, his proposal was an Independent alteration of that idea of ordination held by the Presbyterian Westminster Assembly of 1645, which was accepted in that same year by the General Assembly of the Kirk of Scotland.

b *Fletcher's Plan*

Fletcher sent Benson's letter to Wesley, but Conference only dealt with his first proposal that preachers be tested afresh. However, on 1 August 1775 Fletcher sent Wesley a full plan, advising that first of all, bishops be asked to ordain Methodist preachers. If repulsed, then Wesley could ordain. In 1780 Wesley did make a fruitless appeal to the Bishop of London to ordain. Wesley kept Fletcher's letter carefully. We will indicate how he ignored, corrected, or followed these proposals, but Fletcher's suggestion that after Wesley's death Methodist Moderators should ordain, and also 'overlook' people and preachers, was obviously derived from Wesley's proposal of 1769, and this may have been true of most of his ideas. Wesley's ultimate plan was mainly his own.

CHAPTER EIGHT

Comprehension and Catholicity

a *Choosing Bishops?*

As early as 1769, some American Methodists wanted their own ordinances, and there were American Methodist ordinations on Presbyterian principles in 1779, in which year Wesley said Christ gave the commission to baptize 'only to the apostles, and their successors in the ministry', meaning ordained men. (Works 15, p. 188.) Asbury declared the ordinations invalid. Then American Independence in 1783 made the future of the Church of England there most uncertain. In that year, under Coke's inspiration, the British Conference asked that the term 'Conference' should be defined, so that the right to use Trust properties would be safeguarded after the deaths of the Wesleys. Counsel asked Wesley also to say in a Deed of Declaration 'how the Conference should be governed after his death'.

In February 1784 the Deed was signed, and Wesley also told Coke that Asbury had also asked for 'some mode of church government (for American Methodism) ... That, keeping his eye on the primitive churches ... he had much admired the mode of ordaining bishops which the Church of Alexandria had practised ... (they) would never suffer the interference of a foreign bishop in any of their ordinations; but the presbyters, on the death of a bishop, exercised the right of ordaining another from their own body ... for 200 years.' Drew, who tells this story,

(*Life of Dr. Coke*, p. 62) was an intimate friend of Coke. The historical problem raised for many writers by Coke's appeal in his letter of 9 August to Wesley to ordain him, is solved by accepting the implication of this precedent —that originally Wesley wanted Coke's ordination as Superintendent to take place in *America*.

In the Deed, Wesley left to the Legal Hundred after his death, his powers of episcopé to admit or exclude Methodist preachers and people, giving them wider powers than Fletcher had suggested. In June 1780 John wrote Charles, claiming on the basis of Stillingfleet's *Irenicon* that he had 'a right to ordain'. We will therefore compare Stillingfleet's account of the ordination of their bishop by the presbyters of Alexandria, with the Deed's election of the Methodist President. (i) Conference was 'to *chuse a President . . .* of their Assembly *out of themselves*'. The twelve presbyters 'did *choose out of their number, one to be head over the rest*'. (ii) 'The President shall have such *powers*, priviledges, *and authoritys as the Conference shall* from time to time *entrust into his hands.*' 'This election in Jerome (of the bishop by the presbyters) must imply the conferring *the power and authority* whereby the Bishops acted.' (Ibid p. 274.) This double parallel surely proves Stillingfleet's account of the Alexandrian precedent guided Wesley regarding the election of the President here, and confirms Coke's claim it guided Wesley originally in the method of ordaining the American Superintendent. A further evidence of Stillingfleet's influence is in the following parallel: The *President* 'shall continue such until the election of another President . . . in the next or other subsequent Conference'. 'Whether the *President* (of Calvin's Ecclesiastical Senate at Geneva) should be for life or only by course, they judged it an accidental or mutable thing, but that there should be one, essential and necessary.' (Stillingfleet, ibid p. 407.)

87

b *Wesley's Proposal to Ordain*

Wesley's proposal to ordain, according to Pawson, was first advanced by Wesley in his select committee (at the July 1784 Conference). Pawson, a member, said 'the preachers . . . to a man, opposed it. But *I* plainly saw that it would be done, as Mr Wesley's mind appeared to be quite made up.' (Tyerman, *Wesley*, 3, p. 428.) This Committee met at the end of Conference, which explains why it was not recorded in the Minutes. Moore says it was arranged 'that the Ministers who were to assist Mr Wesley should meet him at Bristol'. (*Life of John Wesley*, 2, p. 332.) I suggest this refers to the ordinations of Whatcoat and Vasey, who would then need a third presbyter in America to ordain Coke as Superintendent. The preachers' opposition probably inspired Coke to write Wesley on 9 August asking '*that the power of ordaining others should be received by me from you*, by the imposition of your hands' as 'my exercising the office of ordination without that formal authority may be disputed'. He also pleads that Wesley should ordain Whatcoat and Vasey. Rankin, formerly General Assistant in America, had said certain clergy would assist Coke in ordaining in America. Coke was justified in doubting this, and wanted to be sure Wesley would stand by his decision, and ordain the two preachers to assist him in ordaining Asbury as Superintendent.

c *Wesley's Revision of the Book of Common Prayer in 1784, 1786, and 1788*

This went far beyond Fletcher's suggestions.

Evidence of Wesley's intention in the American ordinations is in his 'Journal', and 'Diary', his 'Certificate' issued to 'Superintendent' Coke, his 'Letter' (10 September 1784) to the American Preachers, and his 'Sunday

Service', which he commended to them. This last contains the Ordinal for Deacons, Elders, and Superintendents, and Wesley would use all three if he ordained Coke, Whatcoat, and Vasey in September 1784. We must consider its general motive first before assessing the 'Ordinations'.

In June 1942 I argued in the Wesley Historical Proceedings, that Wesley had familiarized himself in Calamy's *Abridgment of Mr Baxter's Life* in April 1754, with the position of many Presbyterians at the Restoration, and his revisions were inspired by regard for that 'Baxterian' Church of England 'which would have comprehended at least his Presbyterian ancestors'. Dr Rattenbury then stressed Wesley's practical desire to have his book widely used among anti-Anglican Americans, and Rev. J. C. Bowmer said Wesley had the same aim in respect to British Methodists. We agree the motive was to comprehend Anglican and Dissenting Methodists. Consequently, Wesley advised his preachers to use the Service, which he shortened,[1] each Sunday, to administer the Lord's Supper weekly, and to read the Litany on Wednesday and Friday, but provided for the lovers of free prayer, by advising extempore prayer (C) on other days, and within the Lord's Supper.

He omitted from Baptism elements implying baptismal regeneration (C:APB), Godparents (C:APB permits parents as sponsors), and the sign of the cross (C:APB permits omission). He adds the mode of sprinkling, which he had accepted from Watts in 1751. He also omitted Confirmation; and 'The Order for Visitation of the Sick' which may be because of the form of the absolution (C:APB omits the special absolution) for he altered the declaratory absolution in the Communion into

[1] C=Paralleled in Calamy: APB is important, but the explanation comes later.

a united prayer of elders and people. However, I am not satisfied with anything so far written about Wesley's attitude to baptism, confirmation, or absolution.

He omitted from the Burial Service prayers which in 1661 were felt to be too hopeful about the fate of the wicked (C). He reduced the number of Psalms (APB), omitting parts improper for Christians (APB), probably influenced by Watts's 'Psalms'. From the Communion he omitted the first two Exhortations (C), Offertory sentences from the Apocrypha (C), and the rubric that communicants should kneel to receive (C). The manual acts were included in all editions, save one American alternative edition. He omitted the ring (C), and 'with my body I thee worship' (C) from 'Matrimony'; Lessons from the Apocrypha (C); Lent (C); and the Athanasian Creed (C:APB).

Wesley read Calamy's book in April 1754. In November 1755 he wrote of 'objections to the Liturgy' of the Presbyterians of 1655–61, 'which some (who never read their works) have now', and which in part he shared. His revision follows Calamy so often, that his influence seems very probable, particularly as in 1784 Wesley was consulting others who favoured Comprehension. The over-riding motive, in the light of which detailed revisions must be interpreted, was Wesley's deep desire for comprehension of different elements of worship, and varying worshippers, within Trans-Atlantic Methodism.

d *Coke's Ordination as Superintendent*

Did Wesley ordain Coke as Superintendent (2 September 1784)? What was his intention? The formula for all his certificates follows the Presbyterian definition of ordination familiar to Benson (see p. 85), and where Benson suggested 'for the *work*', Wesley normally had 'for the office', which was on 'Superintendent' Asbury's certificate issued by Coke. Wesley wrote simply 'as a superintendent' on Coke's certificate, which implies 'office'. His Diary does not say 'inducted', or 'commissioned', but that he 'ordained' Coke. He surely used from the Sunday Service 'The Form of Ordaining a Superintendent', which speaks of 'the office and work of a Superintendent', and closely follows the Anglican Form of 'Ordaining or Consecrating' Bishops, and confers the power to ordain. *Therefore Wesley intended to ordain Coke, who was similarly to ordain Asbury, both to be Superintendents,* who were to be:

(i) *Presidents.* He recommended Coke in his Certificate as 'a fit person to preside over the flock of Christ' (see page 74), as Lutheran Superintendents did over ministers' meetings, and Bishops over Diocesan Councils, and as he had wanted Fletcher to do, 'as one ruler' (see page 84). The Deed of Declaration provided that Conference could entrust the President with further 'powers, priviledges, and authoritys'.

(ii) *Visitors.* The original Scottish Superintendents, like the Lutheran, and like the ideal Anglican bishop, visited the churches, and inspected them, as Wesley, Asbury and Coke had already done. Therefore the special function which distinguished these Methodist from the other Protestant Superintendents was the Episcopal function which Coke put first in May 1787, among his 'priviledges'.

(iii) *'Ordaining . . . presiding . . . and travelling at large.'* (Etheridge, *Coke*, pp. 222–3.) *In Wesley's Ordinal, Superintendents alone admitted Deacons to the first stage, ordaining them without help as did Wesley, and as does a bishop.* This Episcopal power of admission to the ministry is crucial in identifying Wesley's theory. At least three bishops consecrate an Anglican bishop. Two elders shared with the Superintendent in ordaining a Methodist Superintendent, but Coke later said the

Superintendent *must* share, which the Ordinal implies.

e *On What Theory did Wesley Ordain?*

(i) Wesley wrote, '*Lord King's* Account of the Primitive Church convinced me many years ago *that bishops and presbyters are the same order, and consequently have the same right to ordain* . . . I have accordingly appointed . . . Joint Superintendents'. In his *Notes on the New Testament* Wesley stated this in King's, and Stillingfleet's terms, and both, in general, justified presbyteral ordination. Wesley could justify his ordinations of the presbyters Whatcoat and Vasey in part on this basis. Even here, Wesley knew his ordinations were 'irregular', but argued the American need was 'a case of necessity' (Letters 7, p. 262) and was supported by Stillingfleet's claim that presbyteral ordination in 'case of necessity' was valid according to the Church of England (Stillingfleet, ibid., p. 277).

(ii) King's New Testament Bishop presided over one local church: Stillingfleet's Apostle, and Wesley's Superintendent presided over and visited many churches, and was a closer parallel to the Diocesan Bishop, than to the New Testament 'episcopus', or indeed to other Protestant Superintendents. *Wesley needed a theory which, on the basis of the New Testament parity of 'episcopoi' and presbyters, provided, in effect, for a modern return of presbyters to a polity episcopal in form, but avoiding the name 'Bishop'. The full justification of his action was Stillingfleet's theory,* which we found in part in his *Notes on the New Testament*, and which embodied King's.

Once again we are in Alexandria, watching their choice of bishop. Stillingfleet said, 'This election in Jerome must imply the *conferring the power and authority* whereby the Bishops acted'. (Remember the election of President in the 1784 Deed.) 'The first setting up of this power . . .

92

in the Bishop above presbyters . . . Jerome attributes . . . not to any Apostolical institution, but to the free choice of the Presbyters themselves.' (Ibid p. 274.) Stillingfleet said Apostles had wider powers than the local presbyters, and so, 'If the Church sees it fit for some men to have this power (of presbyters) enlarged for the better government in some, and restrained in others, that enlargement is the appointing no new office'. (Ibid., pp. 193–5.) He says that diocesan episcopacy originated historically when all presbyters agreed to relinquish some privileges, that some 'episcopoi' might have wider powers like the apostles. Presbyters were free to do this again. Later we must say why Wesley was so annoyed when American Methodists called their Superintendents 'Bishops'.

(iii) *'Wesley—Apostolic Man'*. This apt title of E. W. Thompson's book expresses a second theory of Coke and Wesley. Coke in his letter of August 1784 pleaded with Wesley to ordain, using 'that power . . . which . . . God hath invested you with'. In the Certificate, Wesley spoke of being 'providentially called' to this act. Coke, in his ordination sermon for Superintendent Asbury in December 1784, justified the ordinations of Superintendents, because of the unanimous vote of the American preachers on the Alexandrian precedent, and because 'the whole body have invariably esteemed this man (Wesley) as their chief pastor'. His extraordinary apostolic and evangelical call of 1739 onwards fused with the 'Catholic' precedent of the first two centuries in Alexandria, and provided a ministry which succeeded in comprehending Anglican and Dissenting members and ministers in America. Some thought this man had aged! Some have said of Wesley's theories, 'You cannot have it both ways'. But comprehensive concern—or universal love—hoped to achieve it.

f *Wesley's wider, 'Catholic' or Ecumenical, Intentions, in using the title 'Superintendent'*

Wesley and Coke both thought a good deal about State Churches in 1784.

First, the title 'Superintendent' was acceptable to *Lutherans*. There were many Lutherans in America. Irish-German Palatinate Methodists contacted them in New York. Coke preached in December 1784, vindicating ordaining Asbury as Superintendent 'on the principles of most of the Reformed Churches in Christendom' and Otterbein, a Presbyterian Lutheran presbyter who later became a 'bishop' in an Evangelical denomination shared in ordaining Asbury as Superintendent. Stillingfleet deals with 'The Judgement of Reformed Divines' (ibid., Pt. II, Chap. 8) instancing Lutheran Episcopacy in Sweden and Denmark, and asserting that German Lutherans with their Superintendents would accept Jerome's position. (Ibid., 411–12.) Wesley met many Lutherans in Saxony in 1738, and later contacted many Lutherans of the State Church of the English Hanoverian kings.

Second, in 1766 Wesley read Knox's own *History of the Scottish Church*, describing the appointment of Superintendents, similar to the Lutheran in jurisdiction, and in 'having no special powers of ordination'. By 1590 presbyteries displaced them. In 1689 ministerial inequality was abolished in this state church, so that ordinations on *King's* theory would have been acceptable in Scotland. Scottish Methodists accepted Wesley's ordinations in 1785.

Third, the title was used in *the English State Church*. Wesley would know both that Bishop Wilson of Sodor and Man was invited to be Superintendent of the Episcopalian Moravians in 1749, and also, through his strong Huguenot contacts, that the Archbishop was Superintendent of a French church in Canterbury which used the English Liturgy, and shared this relation to them in London with the Bishop of London.

This French Protestant acceptance of 'Superintendent' rather than 'Moderator' would be a partial explanation of Wesley's rejection of this latter title which he had favoured in 1769 and Fletcher had advocated in 1775. 'Moderator' travelled from France via Dutch Protestantism to Scotland. Dutch Protestants troubled Methodists in New York, but Wesley established friendly contacts with them on his important visit to Holland in 1783. The Huguenot acceptance of the title 'Superintendent' therefore added to its established wide acceptance.

Fourth, in his Circular Letter to the American Preachers (10 September 1784) Wesley called the Church of England, 'the best constituted National Church in the world'. The Americans took this as a commendation of Episcopacy. He knew that the Lutheran office of Superintendent held by Bishop Jablonski over the Herrnhut Moravians, had prepared for the restoration of their episcopate. Through Olivers, in 1771, he seems to have hinted that he might have considered Anglican consecration. By using the title 'Superintendent', recognized as a Latinized form of episcopus, was he hinting that Methodist Superintendents could become regular bishops? Certainly not—if it would mean they would be 'entangled again with . . . the English Hierarchy', as he said in the same letter. However, was this entanglement inevitable?

If Scottish Presbyterians accepted Superintendents again, and Lutheran Superintendents received special powers of ordination—like American Methodist Superintendents—these would have been steps nearer to 'the best constituted *National* Church in the world' and also to the ideal, '*the Scriptures and the Primitive Church*'. (Letter.)

In principle, although not in detail, this was the vision of the Non-Jurors who taught him to value the Church in all times and places, in their efforts, early in the century, for unity with the Prussian and Hanoverian Churches on the basis of Episcopacy and a revised English Liturgy which they felt would interest 'Lutherans and Calvinists'. (J. Johnson, '*The Unbloody Sacrifice*', II-III, pp. 175–81.)

g *Superintendent and Liturgy for Scotland*

Possibly the Scots heard of the Episcopal claims of American Methodists, for Presbyterian ministers refused Scottish Methodists the Sacraments unless they left Methodism, so Wesley ordained Pawson and two other preachers for Scotland in August 1785, and eight others by 1788. The *Methodists accepted his ordinations, but*, in spite of its Presbyterian revisions, *rejected his 'Sunday Service'*, and so Pawson followed Presbyterian procedure for the Lord's Supper, and in March 1786 was hoping Wesley would not insist on the English forms. In the 1786 Minutes Wesley defended his ordinations for Scotland. It was not separation from the Church of Scotland—'we were never connected therewith: nor from the Church of England; for this is not concerned in the steps which are taken in Scotland'. (For all this see Swift, *Methodism in Scotland*: J. C. Bowmer's, *The Sacrament of the Lord's Supper in Early Methodism*.)

h *Liturgy for Scotland*

Wesley's Revision of the Presbyterian Lord's Supper, for Scotland was not envisaged by Fletcher in 1775.

In 1842, Scottish Methodists demanded that sacraments there be administered 'in strict adherence to the order sanctioned by Mr Wesley, which is the same as that prescribed in the Church of Scotland'. There survives a manuscript of John Braithwaite, Methodist preacher in

Glasgow 1790, ordained by other Methodist preachers in 1797, which contains 'The Order of Administering the Sacrament among the Methodists in Scotland'. My claim is that the original of this Order was drawn up by Wesley with Pawson at the 1786 Conference, and that it shows the Non-Jurors were right at least about some Calvinists' Sacramental views.

Dr G. S. M. Walker of Leeds University has sent valuable parallels to 'Braithwaite' from 'Pardovan's Collections' (1709), which is good evidence for eighteenth-century Presbyterian procedure. The outline of 'Braith-waite' is Presbyterian, and includes Scottish practices —fencing the table, and sitting at the tables, and the Institution and sentences for the Administration taken from Paul. Wesley could have accepted these, justifying the right of Scottish Methodists to follow Presbyterian procedure.

Certain features suggest Wesley composed the original 'Braithwaite'.

(i) Three times, hymns (from 'the sacramental hymn-book') are sung, a Methodist innovation. (ii) 'Braithwaite' says, 'desire the elders to bring forward the elements'. Wesley *may* have tolerated elders in Glasgow from 1787–9, or originally suggested Methodist officials. Dr Walker says this Presbyterian entrance probably derived from the people's offertory in the Primitive Church of bread and wine, and he refers to the Non-Juror Liturgy of 1734! On the basis of this, Wesley in 1736 used a 'Prothesis', or table from which elements were brought to the 'altar' in a similar way. In 1772 he wondered whether to resume all his Oxford rules. (iii) An Epiclesis, or Invocation, was used continuously though not universally, in Scotland from 1600 onwards, and appears in 'Pardovan', echoed in the instruction in 'Braithwaite', 'offer up the prayer of *consecration*', a title given by Wesley to this Presbyterian prayer in 1764. In 'Braithwaite', Paul's words used for administering the elements differ significantly from the A.V. as follows: 'The Lord Jesus *Christ, in* the same night in which He was betrayed, took bread, and when he had *blessed it* (*as I trust He has done this*)...': 'in' may have been added by someone familiar with the Institution in the Book of Common Prayer. At my request, the Rev. J. C. Bowmer confirmed that Wesley's Field Bible (given to Henry Moore in 1788) includes 'Christ' as above, and also omits 'ye' from 'this do ye in remembrance of me' (A.V.) as does the command about the cup in 'Braithwaite'. This fascinatingly confirms that Wesley composed 'Braithwaite', and before 1788.

I have found no similar Presbyterian stress on 'Blessing', but in 1788 Wesley republished his sermon on 'Constant Communion', which says Christ commanded 'the Apostles to *bless* . . . bread', and his 'Notes on the New Testament' on 1 Corinthians 10:16 explain '*blessing*' as 'setting the cup apart to sacred use, and solemnly *invoking* the blessing of God upon it'. Clearly Wesley's Non-Juror inheritance made the Presbyterian use of an Epiclesis very welcome to Wesley. The Sacramental Hymns on the Mixture were probably used by Pawson in Scotland, for just before his death in 1806 he used water and wine in a self-administered sacrament. (iv) 'Dismiss each table with these words, "Go from the Table of the Lord in peace, and may the God of *Love* and *Peace* go with you." ' This was a traditional Scottish Presbyterian and Episcopalian dismissal. 'Braithwaite' gains full significance here from Wesley's 'catholic' and evangelical conception of communion. In response to the Invocation, the Lord now blesses the elements, and offers 'the first blessing' of *peace* through justifying faith, and 'the second blessing' of holiness or perfect *love*.[1] (v) 'Braithwaite' uses Wesley's

[1] See p. 66 regarding Wesley and Methodist Dismissal Sentences.

characteristic word 'subjoin', used in his report of his visit in May 1788 to the Glasgow chapel formerly in Pawson's care. In this he says 'Methodists . . . do not impose any particular mode of worship; but you may continue to worship in your former manner'. (vi) 'Braith-waite' follows Presbyterian precedents in substituting a Doxology for the Gloria, but it is that of Ken, the Non-Juror, often used by Wesley. (vii) May we now say that *Wesley* finally provided for an exhortation to those who had never communicated? Would his acceptance of this full evangelical use of the Lord's Supper partially resolve our dilemma about Open Communion? Why not an Ecumenical Communion Day, on which to invite non-members who believe our Lord could give pardon and power, to come to the Table as a sign they are 'ready and desirous' to become Church members? Methodist historians have patronized or excused the Wesley of 1784 onwards. 'Onwards' it is—towards the twenty-first century.

i *Widening and Narrowing the Separation*

Dr Coke said in 1791 that from about 1782–3 until 1789 he 'promoted a separation from . . . the Church of England'. He 'went farther in the separation . . . in America than Mr Wesley . . . did intend', presumably a reference to his full episcopal claim for the Methodist Church and its Bishops. In the 1786 British Conference he argued that Methodist services should be held in Church hours because all the converted clergy were Calvinists, but Conference only allowed such services when the Minister was wicked, or preached Arian or equally pernicious doctrine, when town churches could only take half the people, or there was no church within two or three miles. Preachers should then read 'part of the church prayers from Wesley's "Sunday Service" to endear the church service' to those who only heard extempore prayer. (Myles, *Chron. Hist.* p. 171.) During the connexional year 1786–7, services were held in Church hours in Scotland as a year's experiment. (Letters 7, pp. 370–1.) Late in 1787 or early in 1788, Coke said some Dublin Methodists were attending Dissenting chapels, so he arranged for Methodist services in Church hours, Methodists to attend on the fourth Sunday for communion at the cathedral, and Wesley eventually accepted this in May 1788.

Charles Wesley disliked the 1786 development, made it clear at Conference, and wrote a friend that for fifty years he had feared schism. John produced his Sermon on 'Schism' that same year. It has at times been expounded almost as a justification of secessions! He rightly says the New Testament word means divisions within a Church, rather than separation from it. Roman and Anglican denunciations of separations from them, solely on the basis of this word, are ill-founded, but 'a causeless separation from a body of living Christians' is evil, and produces evil fruits. One can leave a society which demands what God forbids, or omits what he commands, which, 'blessed be God . . . this is not . . the case' with the Church of England. He strengthens 'Church Methodists', advising others, 'Do not rashly tear asunder the sacred ties which unite you to any Christian society'. He commends 'the peacemaker in the Church of God . . . the God of peace is on your side . . . in due time, thou shalt reap, if thou faint not'.

His Sermon on 'The Church', published at the same time, opens the door into the Church of England wide to those with a living Trinitarian faith. All such 'saints' in a kingdom form a National Church, and all in the world form the Catholic, or Universal Church. He would admit Roman Catholics, and any others with a living Trinitarian faith into the Catholic Church and the Church of England, but its members, 'the saints', must be holy, with love for every child of God, for it is the Holy Catholic Church. Clearly, whilst Coke was working for separation, Wesley was striving to hold together former pagan, Dissenting and Anglican elements in his Societies, and to keep the latter associated with their former denominations. He stated this in his explanation of the principles of Methodism in Glasgow in May 1788: Methodists 'may continue to worship in your former manner'. Methodists must help to unify the Catholic—the Comprehensive—Church of Christ.

CHAPTER NINE

'He, Being Dead . . .'

I   RETURN TO THE ORIGINAL PLAN

ON 29 March 1788 Charles Wesley died. A fortnight later, Wesley broke down when giving out, from his brother's great hymn 'Wrestling Jacob', the lines

> My company before is gone,
> And I am left alone with Thee.

Did Wesley's attempt to bring the Trans-Atlantic Society back to his original plan begin then, in the pulpit in Bolton? Or, in the many discussions he had with Rankin, the Former General Assistant for America, prior to Conference? Wesley had wanted the American Methodists to appoint Whatcoat Superintendent in 1787. They refused, Asbury thinking this a stretch of power. On 16 July 1788 Wesley conferred all morning with Rankin and on 17 July he wrote Whatcoat, 'It is truly probable the disavowing *me* will, as soon as my head is laid, occasion a total breach between the English and American Methodists'. Wesley saw Rankin on six separate occasions, before—

a *The Ordination of Alexander Mather as Superintendent in August* 1788

Pawson wrote (13 December 1793) that Wesley favoured Episcopacy, not Presbyterianism, and 'To preserve all that was valuable in the Church of England among the Methodists, he ordained Mr Mather and Dr Coke bishops. These he undoubtedly designed should ordain others. Mr Mather told us so at the Manchester Conference (1791); but we did not then understand him.' He praised Mather highly as having been Wesley's right-hand man for years. Pawson was President, and Mather was still alive—it is incredible that he lied about the ordination. Myles says Wesley 'ordained' Mather 'Bishop or Superintendent', writing in 1803, six years after being colleague with Mather. Moore says 'Wesley gave to those he ordained the title of Superintendents', surely having Coke and Mather in mind. This three-fold testimony from contemporaries is conclusive—save for the title 'Bishop'.

In September 1788 Wesley wrote Asbury, 'How can you, how dare you suffer yourself to be called a Bishop? I shudder, I start at the very thought. Men may call me a knave or a fool, a rascal, a scoundrel, and I am content; but they shall never by my consent call me Bishop! For my sake, for God's sake, for Christ's sake, put a full end to this!' This must be taken seriously. The title had been changed to 'Bishop', in the American Discipline in 1787, but E. W. Thompson was wrong in saying Wesley intended the title 'Bishop' should be used in America. Wesley reminded Asbury that 'Bishop' was an emotive title, and used all his religious force to persuade him to become a 'Superintendent'.

He continues: 'Let the Presbyterians do what they please, but let the Methodists know their calling better'. This may explain, 'Men shall never . . . call me Bishop', for Wesley was referring to Romans 1:1, 'called to be an apostle', which, he explained in his 'Notes', means 'And made an apostle by that calling. While God calls, He makes what He calls.' Asbury had had this inward call of

God to be an apostolic, itinerating, missionary bishop, not a local, presbyteral bishop. Nor may we forget that in 1771, for the sake of such of his 'evangelists' who needed ordination, Wesley appeared to be ready to consider the outward call of God to him to be a bishop. He felt that it was important in the meantime that on both sides of the Atlantic, it should be understood by Presbyterians and Anglicans that superintendency involved upgrading, but not the full claim to be 'Bishop'.

Clearly Wesley did not consider his subsequent ordinations of Moore and Rankin for England in February 1789 as contradicting this policy. He pleaded with both 'to continue united to the Established Church', and Rankin had already proved his loyalty. Wesley put severe limitations on his ordinations. Preachers ordained for Scotland could not administer sacraments on return to England. Mather was not to ordain till Wesley had died, and apparently then, only in case of necessity, and only the few ministers needed to meet the limited needs defined in 1786.

b *Methodist Expressions of Loyalty to the Church of England*

From March to July 1789, Wesley spent much time unifying Church Methodists and Dissenting Methodists in Ireland on the policy of Church Prayers in Church service hours in the main Dublin Methodist chapel for three Sundays, and communion in the cathedral on the fourth Sunday. In May 1789 he prepared his Korah Sermon 'On the Ministerial Office'. This defended lay preachers as being New Testament 'evangelists', and on Roman and Protestant precedents. Hower, he said evangelists were neither pastors nor priests, and that neither in the New Testament, nor during the first three centuries did evangelists act as pastors or bishops in administering sacraments. The preachers must not 'seek the priesthood'. 'Ye are of no sect . . . are friends to all parties . . . forward all in . . . love of God and man . . . called in the Church of England . . . be Church of *England* men still. Do not frustrate . . . the very end for which God raised you up.'

Coke arrived from America in June 1789. In a letter to Bishop Seabury of the Protestant Episcopal Church in America, on 14 May 1791 (called Letter B in subsequent paragraphs), he said that in 1789 he recanted his error in promoting separation from the Church of England before 3,000 in the largest Methodist chapel in Dublin, repeating it in London and other places in Ireland and England, killing all hopes of separation in both countries. In July, the Irish Conference reaffirmed its intention not to separate, confirmed by an unparalleled Methodist attendance for communion at the cathedral, followed by huge communions at Manchester, and Leeds, where the English Conference was also unanimous against separation. This was no mere formality. Wesley is said to have preached his Korah Sermon at the Irish and British Conferences. In 1793, Creighton, the Church of England presbyter who administered the sacraments at City Road Chapel, London, until 1811, said that Wesley repented with tears that he had ordained any of his preachers, and expressed his sorrow for this at the 1789 Conference. What had happened? The trouble in Dublin was hardly sufficient to account for this.

Seabury was consecrated Bishop for America in November 1784 by the Scottish Bishops, who had strong Non-Juror sympathies. His consecration was not accepted by the American Protestant Episcopal General Convention. We remember Wesley said of his Scottish Ordinations in 1785, that the Church of England was not concerned. Drs Provoost of New York and White of Pennsylvania were consecrated at Lambeth in February

1787, and then, in July 1789, Bishop Seabury's consecration was recognized as valid by the American General Convention, which in October accepted a modified Constitution, and a revised Prayer Book which was to be published in October 1790. Were Coke and Wesley aware of the proposals which led to these developments? In a letter of 24 April 1791 to Bishop White (called Letter A in subsequent paragraphs), referring apparently to the use of the title 'Bishop', and very probably to things he (Coke) had done, Coke said of Wesley 'This I am certain of,—that he is now sorry for the separation'. On 11 December 1789 Wesley wrote 'Farther Thoughts on Separation from the Church of England', also published in the *Magazine* in 1790, saying in it, 'I live and die a member of the Church of England; . . . none who regarded my judgment or advice will ever separate from it'.

In 1790 Wesley's policy seems to have tightened in Scotland. Robert Dall says that in the public street, he declared to hundreds: 'We did not come to oppose, but help the Church; and as a proof of it, we did not intend to preach in Church hours'. Wesley's report of his visit to Scotland is short, and critical, but in letters he says 'he never had such congregations', and 'never saw so much likelihood of doing good . . . there . . . if all our preachers would be Methodists indeed'. By 'help the Church' he meant, or included, the Episcopal Church, now linked with the Church of England by the Protestant Episcopal Church of America! There was now the possibility of a Trans-Atlantic Anglican Unity, and yet with American Protestant Episcopal independence.

On 23 July 1790 Wesley saw Coke for six hours, and wrote letters to the American Conference, which have not survived.

Coke sailed in October for the West Indies, and then on to America for the Conferences in South Carolina, Georgia, North Carolina and Virginia. On 24 April 1791 he wrote Letter A to Bishop White, seeking reunion of Methodism with the Protestant Episcopal Church in America. Charles Wesley himself, and Tyerman and Hockin—Victorian Methodist and High Church historian —as well as our latest historian of Wesley's ordinations, all expose Coke for his ambition. It is sad to end the story so.

a *Regret for Separation in America*

(i) Coke admits he 'went farther in the separation of our Church in America than Mr Wesley . . . did intend. He did . . . invest me, as far as he had a right . . . with Episcopal authority, but did not intend . . . an entire separation'. Wesley did feel 'Bishops' more separatist than 'Superintendents'.

(ii) He says Wesley 'went farther . . . than he would have gone, if he had foreseen some events which followed. And this I am certain of,—that he is now sorry for the separation.' We have seen his sorrow, and some of the events he had not foreseen—American repudiation of his authority and developments in the American Protestant Episcopal Church.

b *Desire for Reunion*

'But what can be done for a reunion . . . to accomplish which, Mr Wesley, I have no doubt, would use his influence to the utmost?' Their combined considerable influence would be fully used 'to accomplish that (to us) very desirable object' if the bishops also showed themselves ready to reunite. No historians have suspected that Wesley would have sought reunion. Why is this not treated seriously? He tells of his and Wesley's efforts to prevent separation. Apparently Coke had said nothing to Asbury. He shrewdly pleads for secrecy.

c *Terms for Reunion, common to Letters A and B*

(i) Ordained preachers to continue to administer the sacraments. Coke did not think 'the generality, perhaps none . . . would refuse . . . re-ordination'. Fletcher in 1775 said Wesley should only ordain those who would accept reordination if offered. When Asbury adopted the title 'Bishop' against Wesley's previous warning, Vasey, one of the two ordained by Wesley with Coke, out of loyalty apparently to Wesley, sought episcopal ordination, and later administered at City Road from 1811 till 1824. Wesley admitted that his ordinations, though justified, were irregular.

(ii) Unordained preachers, unacquainted with learned languages, would like some hope of ordination. How could this be, as the present bishops might agree, but could not tie their successors? Was this a skilful hint that an offer of consecration ought to be voluntarily made? In his important letter of 1780 appealing for ordinations, Wesley wanted Bishop Lowth to waive the language requirement, and we saw that Olivers in 1771, and the title 'Superintendent' in 1784, seemed like similar hinting requests for consecration!

Coke continued, 'Something must be done before the death of Mr Wesley, otherwise I shall despair of success . . . Mr Asbury . . . will be exceedingly averse to it.' But his hope of success had already gone! On 2 March Wesley had died! The Rev. John Richardson altered 'brother' in the committal sentence, saying, 'Forasmuch as it hath pleased Almighty God of His great mercy, to take unto himself, our dear *father* here departed . . .'.

d *Terms for Reunion, in Letter B to Bishop Seabury,*
14 May 1784

(i) 'A solemn engagement to use *your* Prayer Book in all our places of worship on the Lord's Day.' First, turn to pages 89–90, and read 'American Prayer Book' for 'APB'. Many of Wesley's 'Presbyterian' revisions in his 'Sunday Service' are paralleled in the Prayer Book of 1789! Second, in APB a hymn is allowed after the Prayer of Consecration, and another in place of the Gloria, which were typically Methodist innovations! Third, in the Communion Service, our Lord's Summary of the Law could be used: in the bidding 'Let us pray for the whole estate of Christ's Church militant here in earth', the last four words are omitted, and there is a guarded Prayer for the Dead; and the Prayer of Consecration includes Institution, Oblation and Invocation, in that order, following the Scottish Liturgy of 1764, agreeably to 'Antiquity', as Seabury had promised the 'Non-Juror' Scottish Bishops. Coke knew it was Seabury's child, when he called it '*your* Prayer Book'. For all these last features, the Scottish Prayer Book was indebted to the Non-Juror Offices of 1718 and 1734, and Rattray's Office of 1744, all of which had influenced Wesley! The threefold combination in APB of elements Wesley had favoured would have surprised him and made him regret the religious separation.

(ii) 'We would expect to enjoy all our rights as a *Society* in the most exclusive sense, as we do now in Europe . . . the receiving or rejecting members in or from our Classes, Bands, Love-feasts, etc. . . .'. 'Etc.' would include admission to communion through membership, admittance of non- 'Church' members, and the evangelistic values of the itinerant system. This discipline was extremely precious to Wesley. In 1784, Wesley was glad that the English bishops would not govern the American Methodists. The American Protestant Episcopal Church valued the connexion with Canterbury, but claimed independence of all foreign jurisdiction.

(iii) Coke explains that Methodist 'Presbyters and Deacons must be elected by a majority of the Conference before they can be ordained', but Superintendents have a negative voice, for 'A Superintendent only ordains the Deacons; and a Superintendent must make one of the Presbytery for the Ordination of a Priest or Elder'. Wesley had embodied this in his Ordinal in his 'Sunday Service'.

(iv) At last Coke's ambition comes out. The hinted request for consecration is now made explicit. The confidence of unordained preachers regarding their ordination would be overcome 'if the General Convention of the Clergy consented that Mr Asbury, our Resident Superintendent, should be consecrated a Bishop of the Methodist Episcopal Church on the supposition of a reunion'. He himself 'could not *with propriety* visit the American Methodists, possessing . . . an office (in America) inferior to that of Mr Asbury'. The Episcopal Church must guarantee a supply of bishops ad perpetuum. Before we plunge our daggers into this ambitious man we remind ourselves that, so far, every view he expressed in these letters was either held by Wesley or acceptable to him. And what of this last—that the Methodist Societies could absorb Episcopacy into their system? This was at a time when Charles Daubeny and others were advocating extremely High Church ideas of Orders! Wesley's acceptance of Stillingfleet's advocacy of upgrading presbyters to episcopal positions, Wesley's hint in 1771 that for the sake of the Revival he would consider consecration, the hint implied in his use of the title 'Superintendent', compel me to look afresh at this ambitious man, not to consider his subsequent attempts to secure reunion, or to introduce superintendency into British Methodism. He looks to me very much like an apostolic bishop—that is a missionary bishop—of New Testament times, when in 1813, having himself been virtually the Methodist Missionary Society for years, he broke down Conference resistance to his proposed mission to Ceylon by offering £6,000 to launch it, and, an ambitious man of sixty-five years of age, set sail to die on the voyage. God grant more of this ambition—for Mission and for Unity.

His silence about the real inspiration of his peace-making efforts? That seems to me a moral miracle in such a man. He had failed his leader once, but doubtless he had pledged himself to secrecy, and loyally died with his secret unspoken. The whole logic of the development in this lecture leads to this claim—the hand that wrote these letters was the hand of Coke, but the mind was the mind of Wesley. 'And he, being dead, yet speaketh.'

Returning quickly to England, Coke landed in Cornwall in order to reach London more quickly. He learned that the preachers were unlikely even to accept Superinten-dents. The bold ideas of the aged Wesley which might have led more rapidly towards a united Protestantism for Europe and America were too daring for the devoted younger preachers with their intense but narrower vision. Coke, doubtless thinking of the whole legacy of the 'Catholic' Evangelical Wesley, said, 'It is a weight too great to attempt to wield'. The following year the House of Deputies of the American Protestant Episcopal Church rejected a declaration of the House of Bishops favouring Conferences with other religious bodies which might bring 'that union for which our Lord and Saviour so earnestly prayed'.

Wesley had to wait for the twentieth century to realize some of his liturgical ideas. He had to wait a century and three-quarters—until the Archbishop of Canterbury's Cambridge Sermon of 1946—for that offer of Episcopacy which he invited in 1771. Historians cannot give the answers men of genius and of God would give to problems postponed to subsequent centuries. One can point to his trinity of values—holiness or universal love as supreme, faith, and unity—and ask, 'Must he wait for the twenty-first century for that reunion of Protestantism which he believed could hasten the Mission of his beloved Lord to all mankind?'